The
Pinkertons

Also Published by Doubleday & Company, Inc.

DAWN OVER SARATOGA: The Turning Point
of the Revolutionary War

THE MUCKRAKERS: Crusading Journalists
Who Changed America

THE
PINKERTONS

by Fred J. Cook

Doubleday & Company, Inc.
Garden City, New York

Library of Congress Cataloging in Publication Data

Cook, Fred J.
  The Pinkertons.

  SUMMARY: Details some of the most celebrated cases of the famous
detective agency during its 125-year existence.
    1. Pinkerton's National Detective Agency—Juvenile literature.
[1. Pinkerton's National Detective Agency 2. Detectives] I. Title
HV8087.C66   364.12'06'573
ISBN 0-385-07999-0
ISBN 0-385-04203-5 (lib. bdg.)
Library of Congress Catalog Card Number 73–15331

CONTENTS

The
Pinkertons

1

Saving
a President

THE SQUARE-SHOULDERED, pow-
erfully built, bearded man stood on the rear platform of the
sleeping car as the train sped through the black night toward
Washington. Intense eyes in a square, determined face
searched the sides of the track for pinpricks of light that came
to him out of the darkness. The light signals, flashed from
watchers up ahead to agents at points the train was passing,
indicated that the tracks were clear—that there was no threat
as yet to the life of the tall, gangling man who sat inside the
sleeping car, telling jokes in his unforgettable Midwestern
manner.

It was the night of February 22, 1861. Abraham Lincoln,
the newly elected President of the United States, was on his
way to Washington to take the oath of office, and he had
placed his life and safety in the hands of the man who
watched from the rear platform—Allan Pinkerton, the first
great modern detective and the founder of an investigative

dynasty that has remained famous and flourishing to the present day.

There was at the time a serious doubt whether Lincoln, who was to go down in history as one of the greatest American Presidents, would live to reach the White House. To get there, he had to pass through Baltimore, a city seething with Southern agitation and wild talk of assassination.

The outbreak of the Civil War was only a few short weeks away. The Southern states, passions whipped up by the slavery issue, were preparing to secede from the Union in fierce reaction to the election of Lincoln, regarded by them as "a black Republican" and abolitionist, whose election threatened their way of life. One of the most crucial areas in the impending struggle was the state of Maryland. Its territory ringed the national capital on the north, east, and west; if it joined the Southern states, Washington would be isolated in a sea of rebellion, completely cut off from the North.

Actually, Maryland did not secede, but in February 1861 this was by no means certain. The state of Maryland was in many respects more Southern than Northern; it was rife with secessionist talk and plots. Baltimore, its largest city, was the hub of this activity, and the railroad lines that Lincoln had to take to reach Washington all passed through Baltimore. The President-elect's announced schedule called for him to leave one train bringing him from the west, to ride for a mile and a half through Baltimore streets, to walk through a narrow tunnel, and then to board the connecting train that would take him to the nation's capital. No setup could have been more perfect for ambush and assassination.

Historians years later would divide bitterly over the issue of whether the plot against Lincoln's life was real or the product of Allan Pinkerton's imagination, built up beyond all true proportions to enhance his reputation. But the record seems clear: many besides Pinkerton were convinced of the danger, and it was Pinkerton who took the precautions that probably saved Lincoln's life and insured that he would live to guide the nation through the bloody turmoil of the Civil War.

Allan Pinkerton, at the time he was called to investigate the great Baltimore plot, was the head of his own private detective agency in Chicago. Though not the first, he was certainly the most famous of the nation's private detectives. He had founded his agency shortly after 1850, adopting as its symbol a watching eye, the basis of the familiar term "private eye" by which all such agencies were to become known.

Pinkerton gathered about him a corps of skilled "operatives," as he called his detectives. His major business involved protecting the railroads and their express carriers. This relatively new and rapidly expanding mode of transportation carried immense sums of money and valuable cargoes across the nation; and so the railroads and express carriers such as the Adams Express Company and American Express had become the victims of constant pilfering and daring holdups. Pinkerton had solved several of these crimes, and as the result of his railroad contacts he was summoned to investigate the Baltimore plot against Lincoln's life.

On the morning of January 19, 1861, Pinkerton opened a letter in his Chicago office. It was from Samuel Morse Felton, president of the Philadelphia, Wilmington and Baltimore Railroad, and it asked him to come to New York City on a matter of supreme importance.

3

When Pinkerton conferred with Felton, he learned that the railroad official was concerned about many threats from the Baltimore area. Secessionist sympathizers, he had been told, were plotting to blow up rolling stock, bridges, and tunnels, breaking the vital rail link between Washington and the North.

Pinkerton went back to Chicago, mulling over what Felton had told him. On January 27, he wrote a seven-page letter outlining the methods he would use if Felton wished to employ him. His plan involved sending a number of "operatives" into the Baltimore area to infiltrate the secessionist groups. If he were to do this, he pointed out, he did not want his operations made known "to any politician, no matter of what school or what position." Pinkerton didn't trust politicians; he had had too many encounters with the evils of political influence in his early career as a detective in Chicago.

Felton adopted Pinkerton's plan; and, in early February, Pinkerton and several of his agents left Chicago for Baltimore. Timothy Webster, one of Pinkerton's best, and Hattie Lawton were sent to Perrymansville, some nine miles south of Havre de Grace, where Webster had heard "a Rebel company was organizing." Pinkerton himself opened a brokerage office in Baltimore under an assumed name. The office, not entirely by chance, was directly across the hall from that of another stockbroker, a fiery secessionist named Luckett.

Pinkerton soon was hailing Luckett with a cheery "Hello," as they passed each other in the hallway; and, one thing leading to another, as Pinkerton had intended it should, it was not long before the two business neighbors were dining together and exchanging confidences "over a glass."

4

A nondrinker in private life, Pinkerton on the job could consume joy-juice with the best of them. Luckett soon came to like and trust his boon drinking companion, and so introduced Pinkerton to Cypriano Ferrandini, a leader in the plot to kill Lincoln. Ferrandini insisted to Pinkerton that "murder of any kind is justifiable and right to save the rights of the Southern people."

While Pinkerton was gaining the confidence of Luckett and Ferrandini, another agent he had brought to Baltimore, Harry N. Davies, was becoming friendly with a young aristocrat named Howard, who, Pinkerton later wrote, boasted that he "was willing to die to rid his country of a tyrant, as he considered Lincoln to be."

Meanwhile, up at Perrymansville, Timothy Webster had not been idle. He, too, wormed his way into the confidence of plotters and even joined a Confederate cavalry regiment they were organizing. He, too, listened to "wild talk" about the impending assassination. The plotters, he reported, were discussing plans to cut telegraph wires, blow up bridges, and destroy railroad tracks the instant Lincoln was assassinated. Such sabotage would isolate Baltimore and perhaps even lead to a Southern takeover of this key city.

Pinkerton now alerted Felton to the seriousness of the plot he had been sent to investigate. As he later recalled, he reported that "I had no doubt that there would be an attempt to assassinate Mr. Lincoln and his suite by probably not over fifteen or twenty men."

The evidence that such a plot was brewing does not rest on Pinkerton's word alone. In Washington, Brigadier General Charles P. Stone had been given command of a volunteer force raised for the protection of the almost defenseless capital. Stone, too, had heard rumors of plots against the President's life. He later wrote:

"I received daily numerous communications from various parts of the country, informing me of plots to prevent the arrival of the President-elect in the capital. These warnings came from St. Louis, from Chicago, from Cincinnati, from Pittsburgh, from New York, from Philadelphia and, especially, from Baltimore. . . . Many of the communications were anonymous and vague. But on the other hand many were from calm and wise men . . ."

The Baltimore rumbles especially disturbed Stone, and so he sent three detectives to the city. One was to stay with the chief of police, a gentleman whose loyalty was suspect; the other two were to work undercover, independent of the police. The reports that came back to Stone were contradictory. The detective assigned to the police chief reported he had been assured there were no plots; the detectives working in the field reported plots springing up thicker than crab grass. Or, as Stone wrote, they reported they had found "a band of desperate men plotting for the destruction of Mr. Lincoln during his passage through the city, and by affiliating with them, these detectives got the details of the plot."

Stone passed his information to General Winfield Scott, the aging hero of the Mexican War who was then in command of the Union army. Scott put Stone in touch with Senator William H. Seward, of New York, who had been Lincoln's principal rival for the Republican presidential nomination and who was soon to become Secretary of State in the new administration. Seward took such a grave view of the situation that he dispatched his son, Frederick W. Seward, to intercept Lincoln. Seward's letter to Lincoln read:

"My son goes express to you. He will show you a report made by our detective to General Scott, and by him communicated to me this morning. I deem it so important as to despatch my son to meet you wherever he may find you.

"I concur with General Scott in thinking it best for you to reconsider your arrangement . . ."

Young Seward reached Lincoln in Philadelphia on February 21 and gave him the warning. Hardly had he done so when Pinkerton and Felton arrived at Lincoln's quarters and detailed the information they had gathered to Norman Buel Judd, a friend of Lincoln's and the man in charge of the Presidential party. When Judd asked what they recommended, Felton urged that Lincoln change his plans and go quietly to Washington that same night.

Judd predicted that Lincoln would refuse to do this. He had two commitments the next day. Kansas had just been admitted to the Union as a free state, and Lincoln was scheduled to raise the new flag, with its one extra star, during a Washington's Birthday ceremony at historic Independence Hall. Later in the day, he was to travel to Harrisburg, the capital of Pennsylvania, to meet with the state legislature and attend a banquet. It would be bad politics to cancel such appearances.

By now it was ten-fifteen at night, and Pinkerton was determined to get a decision from the only man who could make it—Lincoln. He forced his way through the thinning crowd of well-wishers and office-seekers to Lincoln's room and asked the President-elect to join the conference with Judd.

Some ten minutes later, Lincoln, weary and gaunt from the grueling day, came into Judd's room, and Pinkerton described in detail the assassination plot he had uncovered.

As Pinkerton wrote years later, he warned Lincoln, that if he were given an escort in Baltimore "it would be by a Disloyal police." He declared himself satisfied that "if Mr. Lincoln adhered to the published programme of his route to Washington an assault of some kind would be made upon his person with a view to taking his life."

Lincoln remained silent for several minutes after Pinkerton had finished. Judd asked if he would consider changing his plans and leaving for Washington that very night.

"No, I cannot consent to this," Lincoln replied promptly. "I shall hoist the flag on Independence Hall tomorrow morning and go to Harrisburg tomorrow, then I have fulfilled all my engagements, and if you [addressing Judd], and you, Allan, think there is positive danger in my attempting to go through Baltimore openly according to the published programme—if you can arrange any way to carry out your views, I shall endeavor to get away quietly from the people at Harrisburg tomorrow evening and shall place myself in your hands."

Lincoln did not mention the warning he had already received from Seward, but there can be little doubt that the separate danger signals flashed from two entirely independent sources prompted his decision. After Lincoln had spoken, Pinkerton and Felton began formulating plans to slip the President safely into Washington the following night.

Pinkerton went to see the president of the Pennsylvania Central Railroad and made arrangements for a special train to bring Lincoln from Harrisburg. At the West Philadelphia terminal, Lincoln would transfer to a waiting train of Felton's Philadelphia, Wilmington and Baltimore line on which two sleeping cars would go directly through to Washington during the night, so that Lincoln would not have to leave the train and pass through the treacherous streets of Baltimore.

Leaving nothing to chance, Pinkerton arranged for a professional wire climber of the American Telegraph Company to cut all wires controlled by the Pennsylvania out of Harrisburg the instant the special train departed. This would prevent news from being flashed ahead to Baltimore in case some agent of the plotters happened to be on the alert.

Pinkerton devised a code by which he would let everyone know how the plan worked out. His choice of code words was unfortunate, opening him to later ridicule by small-minded and envious rivals. Pinkerton himself was to be referred to as "Plums," Lincoln as "Nuts," and the telegraph line as "Sumac."

Felton made sure that his railroad would hold the Washington train in the West Philadelphia station until Lincoln was safely aboard. The conductor was given orders not to leave until he received a package addressed to E. J. Allen at Willard's Hotel in Washington. Allen was a pseudonym Pinkerton was to use throughout the Civil War.

Pinkerton dispatched Kate Warne, the first of the female detectives he had employed—a startling innovation at a time when detectives were exclusively male—to rent the two sleeping cars for "a sick friend and party." Then, calling in every operative at his command, Pinkerton spotted his men at danger spots along the route with instructions to flash light signals that he could pick up, assuring him that the track was clear.

The plan worked perfectly. Lincoln slipped out of Harrisburg unnoticed, and at 10 P.M. on February 22, Pinkerton met Lincoln and his companion, Ward H. Lamon, in the gloom of the West Philadelphia train shed, with panting locomotives spewing out gray clouds of acrid coal smoke. Pinkerton escorted Lincoln to the waiting sleeping cars, where Kate Warne carefully drew the curtains and used her feminine charm to distract the curious conductor.

Lincoln, Pinkerton later recalled, was wearing "an overcoat thrown loosely over his shoulders without his arms being in the sleeves, and a Black Kossuth hat, which he told me someone had presented to him." Settling his long form comfortably in the sleeper, Lincoln began to charm the circle around him by telling some of the droll, humorous stories for which he was so famous.

Pinkerton, on this night of nights, was not attuned to the Presidential storytelling and confessed later he could not recall a single yarn that the President had spun. Worried and preoccupied, he took his station on the car platform and watched for the light signals that would tell him all was well.

The switch in plans, the infinite precautions Pinkerton had taken for secrecy, succeeded so well that the trip to Washington was uneventful. Lincoln arrived safely in the capital at 6 A.M. on February 23, and Pinkerton went to Willard's, where he telegraphed Judd and Felton: "Plums arrived with Nuts this morning."

Later in the day, Pinkerton went back to Baltimore. One of

the first persons he encountered was Luckett, the stockbroker whom he had cultivated to learn the details of the plot. Still unsuspecting, not knowing the man with whom he was conversing, Luckett cursed out "the damned spies who betrayed us."

2

The
Young Cooper

ALLAN PINKERTON, the man who insured Lincoln's safe arrival in Washington, was born and brought up in surroundings that might have been expected to produce a major outlaw rather than the outstanding detective of his time.

He was born on August 25, 1819, in a third-floor tenement flat in one of the worst slums of Glasgow, Scotland. His grandfather, after whom he was named, was a blacksmith; his father, William, a handloom weaver who became a trustee of the Glasgow city jail. The Pinkertons lived in an area of narrow, twisting, filthy alleyways, harboring innumerable brothels, infested with footpads. And their tenement flat was not a happy home.

It was filled with the dissension of two families. Allan's father had sired seven children by his first wife; after her death, he married Isabella McQueen, a pretty girl who worked in a spinning mill. William and Isabella had four children, but only the first two, Allan and his brother Robert, survived infancy.

Life in the crowded flat was one of constant turmoil. Inevitably, the older children of the first family resented those of the second, and there was little peace until the older children married and left home.

Allan was only eight years old when his father died, leaving the family impoverished. Allan's mother went back to work in the spinning mill, and he, young as he was, had to quit school and get a job, laboring from dawn to dusk as an apprentice in a pattern-making shop. His salary for this inhuman labor was counted in pennies, and his mother earned little more. They were so poor that Allan remembered in later life the great occasion on which his mother, in a moment of unusual prosperity, had actually brought home a single egg.

This slum upbringing might easily have produced another footpad; but Allan's father had been a strict disciplinarian, and his mother, with whom he was always close, exerted a strong, guiding influence. In addition, he possessed qualities that seem to have been genetic. Even as a boy, Allan Pinkerton was an intense, aggressive competitor—he exuded self-confidence.

When he was twelve, he cut loose from the pattern-making business, which he found "dreary," and apprenticed himself to a cooper—a maker of barrels, kegs, and casks. Six years later, on December 26, 1837, having served his apprenticeship, he received his journeyman's card as a full-fledged cooper.

Allan Pinkerton had inherited much of his blacksmith grandfather's brawn. He was of medium height and had broad, powerful shoulders; his muscular arms could swing a ten-pound hammer for hours without tiring. He was serious, quiet, close-mouthed; but when he did talk, when he became engaged in discussion, friends quickly became aware of the intense blue-gray eyes that never left a man's face.

Ironically, for one who in later and more prosperous years became widely known as a foe of the labor movement, the down-at-the-heels young Allan Pinkerton was a rebel—and quite a violent one, at that. Scotland and England in the late 1830s were caught up in a wave of rebellion that became known as the Chartist movement. This was a revolt by millions of the poor against a caste system that ground them down and doomed them to lives of abject misery.

The Chartists called for universal male suffrage, vote by ballot with no property qualifications, annual parliaments, and equal voting districts to abolish the "rotten borough" system by which rural areas of relatively small population, dominated by a few aristocratic families, wagged the tail of the British lion. The Chartists envisioned these reforms as leading to a utopia in which "all shall have a good house to live in with a garden back or front, just as the occupier likes; good clothing to keep him warm and make him respectable and plenty of good food and drink to make him look and feel happy. . . ."

Allan Pinkerton, an itinerant cooper who had only one old suit and a shoddy pair of shoes to his name, took up the Chartists' cause with the kind of intense, total commitment that was typical of everything he did. On the night of November 3, 1839, he led a group of his fellow Glasgow workers to join an armed band of Chartists seeking to free one of their leaders who was imprisoned in Monmouth Castle in Newport.

Early the following morning this scarecrow army—young workers from the mills, factories, and mines, their clothes in tatters, their weapons scythes, bludgeons, and an occasional old musket—swept down from the surrounding hills into the streets of Newport. The authorities, tipped off in advance about their approach, had set a trap. The King's 42nd Foot, hidden behind shuttered windows facing the town square, waited until the mob was tightly packed before their gun sights, then blazed away. It was a slaughter.

Allan Pinkerton and his companions, lucky enough to get away, fled back into Glasgow "by the back streets and the lanes, more like thieves than honest workingmen."

The tragic experience did nothing to cool the ardor of Allan Pinkerton. Throughout his life, he was to be one of the world's most stubborn men—a trait that was invaluable in his later investigative career because, once he took out after a man, he never gave up. What is a virtue in one phase of life becomes a flaw in different circumstances, however, and this very stubborn quality was almost the young Pinkerton's undoing.

The Chartists split into two factions: one advocated obtaining their objectives by peaceful, legitimate means, the other was wedded to the idea that reforms could be achieved only by fighting. Pinkerton sided with the militants, and so became in time a marked man.

In the winter of 1842, king's warrants were issued for the arrest of the more violent Chartists. Pinkerton's name was on the list, but when police sought him out in the miserable tenement where he still lived with his mother, they found that he had fled.

"I had become an outlaw with a price on my head," Pinkerton later said.

He hid out for weeks in Glasgow, moving from place to place, sheltered by friends. Before beginning this underground life, he had met a pretty young singer, Joan Carfrae, a book-binder's apprentice who sang at many of the Chartist rallies. Joan and Allan had fallen deeply in love; and when he disappeared in his hide-and-seek existence, she sought out his friends in the coopers' union and begged them to take her to Allan. They did. When the lovers met, Joan agreed to go with Allan to America.

They were married secretly in Glasgow on March 13, 1842; and on the night of April 8 they were smuggled aboard a vessel sailing for Canada. Pinkerton paid for their passage by signing on as the ship's cooper.

A stormy four-week voyage across the Atlantic Ocean brought them to the mouth of the St. Lawrence River off Nova Scotia. Here their vessel, caught in floes of pack ice, was swept upon hidden rocks and began to fill with water. The Pinkertons and other passengers took to the lifeboats and rowed to safety.

It was the latter part of May, 1842 before they reached Montreal. Their only assets were the clothes on their backs and, as Pinkerton later wrote, "our health and a few pennies."

3

The Making
of a Detective

THE PINKERTONS had not been long in the new world before they were drawn to Chicago, a raw frontier town of about twelve hundred inhabitants, filled with the sounds of bawling cattle, its streets a morass of mud. Their stay in Chicago was brief. Pinkerton heard of a settlement named Dundee, founded by Scots immigrants on the beautiful Fox River about fifty miles northwest of Chicago.

In the spring of 1843, he decided to set up a cooperage business in Dundee for the thriving farms in the vicinity. He left Joan with friends in Chicago, promising to send for her the instant he had a shelter in which they could live.

As Pinkerton later recalled, Dundee at the time "was a fair and lovely spot, with its murmurous rivers, splendid farms, noble hills, sunlit valleys and opulent herds in the district." Joan, in later years, was to recall their life in Dundee as "the bonniest days the Good Father gave me in all my life . . ."

Pinkerton quickly found an ideal spot for his business on the rise of a small hill about three hundred yards from a bridge over the Fox River. Here he built a one-story cabin and a nearby workshed, and hung a sign that read: "Allan Pinkerton, Cooperage."

He prospered, working from dawn to dusk—sawing, hammering, and making the barrels, casks, and tubs needed by the farmers of the district. He was so busy and so industrious that he developed work habits that were to stay with him the remainder of his life: to bed at eight-thirty; up at four-thirty; work until dark seven days a week.

There was in all of this no hint that a great detective was about to be born. Allan Pinkerton was a prosperous cooper; and, except for a one-in-a-million chance, it seemed that he would remain so for the rest of his life. Then came the summer of 1847, and the one-in-a-million longshot changed everything.

Lumber was getting low in the yard around the cooperage, and Pinkerton decided to get a new supply. On a small island in the Fox River he had found trees that were ideal for making hoops, staves, and poles. He poled a raft across to the island and spent the morning cutting a supply of wood for his business. He was about to leave when he stumbled upon the remains of a cooking fire.

Pinkerton began to think. In the frontier life of those days, there was no picnicking; people had no time to waste on such frolics. It followed, Pinkerton reasoned, that whoever had built the fire must have been hiding out or using the island for no good purpose.

Though it was no business of his, Pinkerton was curious,

and he began to extend his working hours, slipping over to the island at night and keeping watch for whoever was using the campsite. It was not long before his vigilance was rewarded. Late one moonlit night, he heard the sound of oars and saw a rowboat bringing a number of men to the island, where they landed and started a fire.

Pinkerton now informed the sheriff of Kane County of his suspicions; and, a few nights later, when the mysterious men again returned to the island, Pinkerton and the sheriff headed a raiding posse that corralled a band of counterfeiters along with "a bag of bogus dimes and the tools used for their manufacture."

The success of this first venture in law enforcement made Pinkerton something of a local celebrity, and before long he was asked to use his talents again. H. E. Hunt, the operator of a general store, summoned him and asked him to investigate a mysterious, well-dressed stranger who had ridden into the village, asking directions to "Old Man Crane's place."

Frontier towns like Dundee were often flooded with counterfeit bills in those days, and the merchants who took them were victimized. The man Crane, for whom the stranger asked, had often been suspected of dealing in spurious currency, but there had never been any proof. Hunt's suspicions aroused again by the arrival of the well-dressed newcomer asking for directions to Crane's home, and the merchant suggested that Pinkerton should undertake an investigation.

Pinkerton protested that he was a cooper, not a detective, but Hunt replied: "You helped to break up the 'coney men' and horse thieves on Bogus Island. We're sure you can do work of this sort if you only will."

One of the strongest traits in Pinkerton's character was thus challenged—his supreme self-confidence, a conviction that he could do almost anything he attempted. And so he finally agreed to try his hand at this novel, new profession that was literally being thrust upon him.

Hunt told him that the stranger was having his saddle repaired at a nearby harness shop; and Pinkerton, barefoot and in overalls, strolled over to the harness maker's. He was there, admiring the horse and patting his flank, when the stranger came from the local tavern and mounted to go on his way. Pinkerton, who was always to have a sharp eye for a man's features and bearing, noted that this first suspect was about sixty-five, gray-haired, with a swarthy complexion and keen gray eyes. He wore a gold ring on a finger of his left hand.

As the stranger mounted his horse, he glanced down at Pinkerton, who looked like any village rustic, and asked for directions to "Crane's place." Crane lived in Libertyville, about thirty-five miles away, and Pinkerton told the man exactly how to get there. While giving directions, he pretended that he thought Crane was one of nature's noblemen, calling him a right one, "as good as cheese."

The stranger seemed to value a man who held such a high opinion of Crane, and one word after another led to quite a conversation. It ended with the visitor asking Pinkerton to meet him later in a ravine outside Dundee.

At this rendezvous, the sharp-eyed stranger questioned Pinkerton closely. Pinkerton knew there was no sense in lying— up to a point. He said frankly that he was the town cooper, a fact that he knew the stranger could easily establish for himself. The trouble was, Pinkerton added, departing from the truth a bit, that hard money was difficult to acquire, and he was looking for "a good scheme" that would bring in some ready cash.

Recognizing a kindred soul, the stranger finally confided that he was John Craig, a farmer from Fairfield, Vermont, and he said that he and Crane had "done a great deal of business together."

From this point, Pinkerton led the conversation into a discussion of the nature of "the business." Craig finally said that he would let Pinkerton have fifty ten-dollar bills for 25 per cent cash. The deal was to be consummated in the unfinished basement of the Elgin Academy situated on a hill overlooking East Elgin. Pinkerton trudged back into Dundee and got the money for the transaction from Hunt and another store owner, I. C. Bosworth.

When Pinkerton later met Craig in the basement of the academy, he found that he was dealing with a wary man. He gave Craig $125 in cash, whereupon Craig asked him to leave the basement for a few minutes. When Pinkerton returned, he found the counterfeit bills he had been promised waiting for him under a rock.

It was, he knew, no good. To make a legal case against Craig, he would have to catch the man with the counterfeit money on him. And so, pretending to be delighted with this first deal, Pinkerton arranged with Craig for a larger and more worth-while transaction. They set a date to meet in Chicago; this time, when Craig turned up, loaded with his bogus money, he was arrested by Pinkerton and a waiting Cook County deputy sheriff before he could get rid of it.

Craig was turned over to Kane County authorities for prosecution. Pinkerton testified before the grand jury, and Craig was indicted. Shortly afterward, he escaped from the local jail, "leaving behind [as Pinkerton later recalled] a certain law officer much richer than he had been."

This was the future detective's first lesson in official corruption. It was also the case that changed his life. He found that playing detective was a much more exciting and fascinating business than knocking casks and barrels together in the cooperage at Dundee.

Pinkerton had been bitten by the detective bug the way some men are bitten by the presidential bug; and life was never to be the same again.

4
Founding the Agency

THE ARREST of counterfeiter John Craig put Allan Pinkerton's feet on the path that was to lead to the founding of the most famous private detective agency in America.

It was a lawless time, and Chicago and northern Illinois were still very close to the frontier. Horse thieves, counterfeiters, bank robbers, holdup men, armed thugs of every description infested what was still a wild and undisciplined country; the man who had the courage, integrity, and skill to battle such cutthroats was a rare individual indeed. Pinkerton was just such a one, and his fame quickly spread from Dundee to Chicago.

Joan would have been happy to spend the rest of her life in Dundee, but her husband, as she later said, was "a restless one." When the sheriff of Cook County offered Pinkerton a deputyship, he grabbed at the opportunity, sold his cooperage business, and moved back to Chicago. The straggling town he had left only a few years before was mushrooming with lightning speed into the major city and hub of commerce in the Midwest. Its boom-town atmosphere spawned gangs of desperate outlaws, and Pinkerton, in battling them, soon established his reputation as a tough and fearless agent of the law.

The official corruption for which the so-called Windy City on Lake Michigan has always been notorious soon disgusted Pinkerton, however, and about 1850 he decided to form his own private detective agency. Other lawmen in other cities had gone this route before him, but none had ever achieved the phenomenal success that was soon to be Pinkerton's.

The principal reason for Pinkerton's meteoric rise was that he happened to be the right man with the right idea at the right time. The new railroad lines, in their thrust across the vast reaches of a largely untamed continent, had outstripped the protection of the law. Law enforcement was primitive at best, corrupt at worst. It was also hampered by jurisdictional limitations. City police ran out of authority at the municipal boundary line; county officials, at the county border. There was no centralized law enforcement, and train robbers who looted an express car in one jurisdiction were soon safe in another.

Then came Pinkerton. He and his "operatives" pursued criminals across city, county, and state lines; and when they had tracked their quarries to earth, they enlisted the aid of the local law in making arrests. To the railroads of this chaotic era, Pinkerton was a godsend—carrier after carrier contracted with him to protect its lines from the swarming legions of desperadoes.

It was, of course, inevitable that the man who posed such a danger to the lawless ran the risk of losing his own life. Pinkerton received many threats, and one attempt at assassination almost succeeded.

One September evening in 1853, Pinkerton left his office and started to walk along Clark Street toward his home on Adams Street. He was deep in thought; unconsciously, as was his habit, he put his left hand and arm behind his back and under his coat—an uncomfortable position, one would think. However, old pictures always show Pinkerton stowing that left hand somewhere, either behind him or across his chest under the lapels of his coat.

The habit on this occasion almost certainly saved his life. For, as he walked along, a gunman came up from behind and shot him at so close a range that Pinkerton's coat was set afire. Two heavy slugs shattered the bone of his arm five inches above the wrist, then slithered along the bone to the elbow. A surgeon later cut out the slugs and cleansed the wound of torn pieces of cloth that had been carried into it by the powerful bullets. The gunman escaped; Pinkerton recovered and continued his relentless pursuit of underworld desperadoes, undeterred by this narrow brush with death.

Aided by the financing of the railroads and express companies, he rapidly expanded his agency. He had a knack for finding skillful men. His first employee—and one of the wisest selections he ever made—was George H. Bangs, a tall, slender man with a bushy beard. Bangs traced his ancestry back to the *Mayflower;* he was as tenacious on the trail of a wrongdoer as Pinkerton himself, and he soon became Pinkerton's office manager.

Timothy Webster, an English-born police sergeant in New York, caught Pinkerton's eye and joined the agency. So did two other Englishmen who, like Webster, were to play prominent parts in the Civil War spy dramas, Pryce Lewis and John Scully. And then there was Kate Warne.

One afternoon in 1856, Pinkerton's secretary told him that a young woman wished to see him. The visitor was slender and brown-haired; as Pinkerton later wrote, she was "graceful in her movements and self-possessed. Her features, although not what could be called handsome, were decidedly of an intellectual cast . . . her face was honest, which would cause one in distress instinctly [*sic*] to select her as a confidant. . . ."

Kate Warne explained to Pinkerton that she was a widow—and then she surprised him with an astounding proposal. She wished to become a detective and work for his agency.

This was an incredible suggestion at the time. There had never been a woman detective in America, but Mrs. Warne argued that she could "worm out secrets in many places to which it was impossible for male detectives to gain access."

Impressed by the determined widow, Pinkerton mulled over her proposition for a good part of the night; the more he thought about it, the more he liked the idea. The following day, when Kate Warne returned, Pinkerton hired her. He never had cause to regret the move. A few days later, when he assigned her to her first case, "she succeeded far beyond my utmost expectations," he later wrote, and he added: "Mrs. Warne never let me down."

This early in his career, Pinkerton drafted a set of rules for his "operatives" that have remained the guidelines for Pinkerton's, Inc., ever since. The basic idea was that Pinkerton's would always be on the side of the law.

The agency would not represent a defendant in a criminal trial except with the knowledge and consent of the prosecutor. The agency would not shadow jurors or investigate public officials. It would not accept employment by a political party. It would not report on union meetings unless they were open to the public (a hands-off policy that was to be more honored in the breach than in the observance in the tumultuous period after the Civil War). The agency also would not work for antivice crusaders nor would it accept extra gratuities or rewards for its services. It would never investigate the morals of a woman except in connection with a criminal case and therefore would not involve itself in divorce cases, a rule that the agency has followed rigidly ever since.

This formative Chicago period was important in Pinkerton's later life. As a result of his protective work for the railroads, he met two men who were soon to become national figures. One was the handsome, dashing George Brinton McClellan, the vice-president and chief engineer of the Illinois Central Raiload, a man who was soon to become one of the first important Northern generals of the Civil War. The other was Abraham Lincoln, then an attorney who handled many railroad cases.

There was still a third personality with whom Pinkerton became fascinated and whom he idealized beyond all reason. This was John Brown, the fanatical abolitionist who helped precipitate the Civil War by his raid on the federal armory at Harpers Ferry in what is now West Virginia. Brown was to die on the gallows as a result, but he remained for Pinkerton, contrary to history's verdict, a great man and a noble martyr.

As he later wrote in his book, *Spy of the Rebellion,* Pinkerton was a dedicated abolitionist. "I detested slavery," he wrote, and believed "it to be the curse of the American nation."

During his stay in Dundee, Pinkerton's home had become a stop on the Underground Railroad, that network of ardent abolitionists who harbored escaping slaves and passed them along from post to post until they crossed the border into Canada. Committed as he was to this cause, Pinkerton didn't hesitate when John Brown came to him for aid in the winter of 1859.

Brown, after a raid along the Missouri border, had led a wagon train of his followers and eleven escaping slaves across the snow-swept, frozen prairies. Public sentiment had been aroused against Brown after one of his followers had murdered a prosperous Missouri farmer and made off with the victim's horses, cattle, and wagons. Posses formed to track down the old abolitionist, but Brown was always more ready to fight than his pursuers. They paled and fell back at the threat his armed band presented—and so let him go. Finally, Brown loaded his band and the slaves into a railroad boxcar, and in the early morning of March 11, 1859, he knocked at Allan Pinkerton's Adams Street door.

Pinkerton brought the half-starved slaves into his kitchen, where Joan, roused from sleep, gave them breakfast. Then Pinkerton, acting fast, distributed the refugees among the homes of abolitionist sympathizers who, he knew, would be willing to take the risk of sheltering and protecting them. But the question remained: How was he to get Brown and the escaped slaves out of town?

Pinkerton undertook to solve the problem in his usual self-confident manner. "There is a Democratic meeting in the city today," he told Brown. "I'll go down and make them give me enough money to send you and these slaves to Canada."

The gathering to which Pinkerton referred was the Chicago Judiciary Convention, whose members, unaware of what was being planned for them, gathered under the misapprehension they were to caucus just to select a candidate for judge. Pinkerton disrupted the session, barging into the convention hall holding "a subscription list" he had already drawn up. Bluntly he outlined the situation, and bluntly he informed each man just what was expected of him.

If the politicos refused to contribute, Pinkerton said, he would bring John Brown himself before them; and if any United States marshal tried to arrest Brown, Pinkerton would not guarantee the consequences. Almost certainly, there would be violence.

Not relishing this prospect, the politicians came forward one by one and dropped their contributions into Pinkerton's receptive hat. Within a few minutes, he had collected between five and six hundred dollars, a sum that was much more impressive then—in the era of five-cent beer—than it is today.

Late that same afternoon, Pinkerton escorted Brown and his party to a waiting railroad train. The detective carried a pistol under his coat, and he was accompanied by his son William and one of his "operatives." Brown, before he left, hinted at the raid on Harpers Ferry that he was planning; but

Allan Pinkerton, though a champion of the law, still had a bit of the rebellious Chartist in him, and he was not appalled by the idea. Despite his bloody deeds, Brown remained a truly towering figure to worshipful Allan Pinkerton. He indicated this to his son as they stood and watched the train chug out of the station, carrying Brown and his freed slaves to safety.

"Look well upon that man, Willy," Pinkerton told the boy. "He is greater than Napoleon and just as great as George Washington."

This was a fantastic misreading of reality; but then, it was no more inaccurate than some of Pinkerton's estimates of Confederate strength were soon to be.

5

Spying for the Union

THE OUTBREAK of the Civil War plunged Allan Pinkerton into a new role, one he later described in his book, *Spy of the Rebellion*. Pinkerton became a spy at the behest of a man he was to idealize out of all proportion, just as he had John Brown. This second unblemished hero in Pinkerton's private Pantheon was General George Brinton McClellan, who had been given command of the Department of the Ohio.

Pinkerton reported to McClellan at Cincinnati and set up a secret service for the Western armies, adopting for himself the cover of "Major E. J. Allen," with his true name "known only to General McClellan."

McClellan wanted information "on the general feeling of the people residing south of the Ohio River in Kentucky, North Carolina, Mississippi and Louisiana." To get the data McClellan wanted, Pinkerton adopted a disguise and went behind the loosely drawn enemy lines.

He posed as "a gentleman from Georgia," driving "a splendid bay" as he made his way through the Southern states. He had several close calls and once was almost given away by a German barber whom he had known in Chicago. But he performed his perilous mission successfully and returned to Cincinnati, supplying McClellan with page upon page of minute detail about the situation across the Ohio.

The mountainous area of what is now the state of West Virginia (then a part of Virginia) was rife with Union sentiment and weakly held by the Confederates. Pinkerton noted that "there are fifteen hundred troops in the Kanawha Valley, about one thousand near Charleston . . . and about five hundred at the mouth of the Coal below Charleston . . . there are only fifty soldiers at the Red House . . . they had little ammunition at either of the above places . . . the soldiers are equipped with muskets and poor rifles and with the exception of the Kanawha Rangers (100 strong) were very poor specimens of mortality, many of them not exceeding fifteen years of age . . ."

McClellan, preparing to send Union forces into West Virginia, wanted to keep in constant touch with developments there, and Pinkerton decided to send Pryce Lewis on a tour of the Southern states. The English-born Lewis still retained traces of his original accent, and Pinkerton planned for him to become a spy in the grand style, posing as an English lord. Since Lewis had been brought up near the estate of a Lord Tracy, it was decided that he should pretend to be one of Tracy's sons.

Pinkerton always insisted that a disguise must be perfect down to the minutest detail. His Chicago office was always

34

filled with all manner of wigs, garments, and personal trinkets needed to perfect the appearance of his "operatives" in their manifold impersonations. And so now he paid close attention to the trappings that would lend conviction to Pryce Lewis's performance as "Lord Tracy."

He bought a coach "with a spacious boot" and a team of the finest bay horses he could find. A George III vintage English army chest was strapped on behind the vehicle, where it would show to convincing advantage. The "boot" of the coach was stocked with several boxes of the best imported champagne, fine "segars," and a case of port—the luxuries an English lord might be expected to take with him to insure pleasurable hours.

Pryce Lewis was decked out from head to toe in the fashion-plate style of the English aristocracy. He wore a gleaming stovepipe hat. His suit was of the finest broadcloth "of the latest English style." His shoes were of Russian red leather. His purse "bulged with an abundance of English sovereigns," and he carried "a handsome segar case with the British lion in ivory conspicuously embossed on it." To add a final and convincing touch, Pinkerton handed over to this bogus "Lord Tracy" his own gold watch and chain, together with a diamond ring to flash on the finger of one hand.

Sam Bridgeman, another of Pinkerton's agents, was assigned the role of footman to the new English "lord." Bridgeman, who had been born in Virginia and still retained his southern accent, "handled the reins in a style worthy of a turnout in Pall Mall or Piccadilly."

Pinkerton gave the pair a final inspection on the evening of June 27, 1861, then sent them off on a riverboat that would take them on the first stage of their journey behind Confederate lines. Theirs was to be one of the most daring and hazardous spy adventures of the war.

On the road to Sulphur Springs by way of Charleston, the two Pinkerton spies were stopped by a Confederate cavalry patrol. The suspicious cavalrymen took Lewis to a farmhouse, where he was questioned by a Colonel Patton—the grandfather of the famous World War II general. Lewis, a glib talker, convinced Patton he was the genuine article—a young, titled Englishman making a tour of the South, curious to learn what he could firsthand about the courageous, rebelling Southern states. Lewis and Patton shared some bottles of champagne that Sam Bridgeman brought from the silver-embossed boot in the carriage; and Patton, under the influence of the wine, took Lewis on an inspection tour of his fortifications, which, he said, he could hold against ten thousand Yankees for ten years.

Lewis's deception of the colonel appeared to have worked to perfection; but perhaps Patton, after the fumes of the champagne had worn off, retained some small residue of doubt. In any event, he insisted that "Lord Tracy" must be questioned by General Henry A. Wise. At this news, Lewis later said, "I thought the hair on my head was standing straight up." He had reason to feel apprehensive. Wise had the reputation of a ferociously tough soldier; it was he, indeed, who had sent John Brown to the gallows.

Wise questioned Lewis in "a savage manner," evidently suspicious of any English "lord" who would embark on a pleasure jaunt through a countryside at war. It seemed for a moment as if Wise would have both Lewis and Bridgeman arrested on suspicion, but Lewis brazened it out. He was the perfect picture of an angry and highly insulted young Englishman. He even threatened to go over the general's head and appeal to the British consul in Richmond, a bold bluff that seems to have convinced Wise he probably was "Lord Tracy." And so, in the end, the Confederate general let the Pinkerton spies go.

Though they had escaped from the shadow of the gallows, Sam Bridgeman was unnerved by the experience. He wanted to abandon the whole trip and flee back toward the Union lines. Lewis, made of sterner stuff, realized that such a move would be a dead giveaway and that Confederate cavalry would come pounding after them. Their only chance was to continue their itinerary just as if nothing had happened.

There was nothing Lewis could do, however, to restore the shattered nerves of Sam Bridgeman. For the nineteen days of their journey, Lewis had to contend not only with his own fears, but with the weeping, trembling, hand-wringing shadow of his companion. Bridgeman became ever more of a problem. He cringed at the first sign of danger. Every night he wept and moaned over his wife and children, whom he might never see again. For solace, he tipped the bottle more and more frequently, becoming so drunk on occasion that his loose and wagging tongue threatened to give them away.

The hazards faced by a spy deep in hostile country are, at best, enough to test the nerve of the stoutest. Pryce Lewis later wrote that he came to feel suspicious eyes upon his back wherever he went, and he had to resist the impulse to keep looking over his shoulder to see if he was being pursued. Added to this normal apprehension, he had the burden of

Sam Bridgeman, draped about his neck like an albatross. It was almost more than a man could be expected to bear, but Lewis proved equal to the task.

He lived his role of unconcerned English lord to the hilt. He told one group of Confederate volunteers that England's "iron clad fleets" were ready to "thunder" across the ocean to help the Southern cause. In another town, he delivered a lecture on the Crimean War and again predicted that Britain would intervene to help the rebelling Southern states. He was such "a fine speechifier," as one of his Southern listeners called him, that he carried out his precarious mission with a flourish; and on July 18, he got himself and Sam Bridgeman safely back to Cincinnati.

The information he had gathered was of the greatest importance. McClellan, recognizing its value, ordered Pinkerton to send Lewis at once to General Jacob D. Cox, then in command of Union forces near Red House on the Kanawha River.

Lewis told Cox that General Wise had only about fifty-five hundred soldiers in his command. He enumerated the number of artillery pieces available to defend Charleston, now the capital of West Virginia. He told Cox that a quick Union advance would encounter opposition only at the junction of the Coal Mouth and Kanawha rivers and at the Elk Suspension Bridge. Cox "appeared astonished" at this information.

Cox probed cautiously at the Confederate front, and Wise, after a bloody skirmish, fell back from the junction of the Coal Mouth and Kanawha, burning the bridge behind him. Colonel Patton, wounded, was taken prisoner.

This quick and relatively easy victory should have triggered a swift pursuit of the enemy; but that evening Lewis, who had accompanied the attacking force, returned to headquarters to find Cox much upset. The general told him that "two good Union men, Virginians," had just come in and reported that Wise, at the head of a formidable army of sixty thousand men, was entrenched on the road to Charleston. Lewis knew that this could not be true. He denounced the "two good Union men" for spreading "a falsehood" intended to deceive Cox.

"I warned you, General, you would have two good fights, one at the Coal Mouth and the other at the Elk Suspension Bridge," Lewis reminded Cox. "Your men have forced the Rebels to evacuate the Coal Mouth, which Colonel Patton predicted he could hold for ten years. The bridge is burned, and Colonel Patton is a prisoner in your hands."

"That is true, Mr. Lewis; that is true," the general agreed.

All right, said Lewis, this should demonstrate that his information had been good, and he wanted to make a prediction: "I promise you that, with the men you have here, you could be in Charleston within twenty-four hours."

Cox was convinced. The next morning, he ordered his troops to advance. Lewis, his mission performed, returned to Cincinnati, and he had hardly reached the city when the word was flashed from the front that Cox had taken Charleston. Wise was in full retreat into the mountains, and the entire state of West Virginia was in Union hands. The first real wedge had been driven into the Confederate front in the border states—a victory made possible largely by the information that Pinkerton's "Lord Tracy" had gathered behind enemy lines.

6

Rebel Rose

IN THAT SAME MONTH of July 1861, when Pryce Lewis was helping to save West Virginia for the Union, a beautiful Confederate spy in Washington was sending south the information that would insure one of the worst Northern disasters of the war—the rout of the Army of the Potomac in the first Battle of Bull Run.

Washington was the nation's capital, but for decades its social life had had a distinctly Southern flavor. Belles from Virginia and Maryland, ardent in their Southern sympathies, were the foremost hostesses of the capital city; their beauty, brains, and social graces bewitched Army and Navy officers, Congressmen, Senators—and at least one President.

Even General Scott's military aide, Colonel E. D. Keys, later acknowledged that he had "found great delight with the Southern damsels, and even with some of the matrons, notwithstanding the incandescence of their treason." The most "delightful" of these dangerous Southern sirens was a tall and striking widow, with flashing dark eyes, a straight and well-formed nose, and thick lustrous black hair. She was Mrs. Rose O'Neal Greenhow, "reputed to be the most persuasive woman that was ever known in Washington."

Rose Greenhow and Allan Pinkerton were now to engage in a duel of wits, top spy against top spy, a match-up unsurpassed in the record of espionage.

Following his success in the West, McClellan was called to Washington to reorganize the shattered army that had thrown away its weapons and fled headlong from the field of Bull Run. He immediately sent out a call for "Major E. J. Allen" to join him and head up the secret service of his new command. The need was great.

The capital was infested with Confederate spies—the most dangerous of all, Rose Greenhow. The widow was forty-four years old at the time, a fading rose, indeed; but so great had been her beauty and charm that she could still addle the wits of men and play upon their passions. She had been born in Montgomery County, Maryland, just outside Washington; in her teens she had been the belle of belles at every Washington ball. She had eventually married a considerably older, but still handsome man, Dr. Robert Greenhow; and their home on H Street had become famous for elaborate dinners and receptions, attended by the foremost figures in Washington.

Jefferson Davis, who was to become President of the Confederacy, had been a friend in those prewar years. So had John C. Calhoun, the powerful U. S. Senator from South Carolina and author of the doctrine of states' rights that was to lead to the Civil War. Rose Greenhow had regarded Calhoun almost as a father; she sat by the aged Senator's death-bed and closed his eyes when he died.

Rose's husband was killed in an accident in California in 1857 while on a mission for the State Department, but his death had not diminished her influence. Rose had always been on friendly terms with bachelor statesman James Buchanan, who wrote her letters signed "your ancient and devoted friend" while he was in London as U. S. Ambassador to the Court of St. James. After Buchanan became President in 1857, the same year in which Rose's husband was killed, he became a frequent caller at the Greenhow mansion, disregarding the tradition against presidential visits to private homes. So constant and obvious were Buchanan's attentions that the New York *Herald* referred acidly to Mrs. Greenhow as "Queen of the Rose Water Administration."

With the outbreak of war, the devastating lady widened her circle of conquests. She later wrote: "I employed every capacity with which God has endowed me, and the result was far more successful than my hopes could have flattered me to expect." Since Mrs. Greenhow was famed for her beauty, imagination does not have to work overtime to visualize some of the "capacities" she utilized. And the flaming love letters written by one of her most important and most highly placed admirers leave even less room for doubt.

This ardent gentleman signed his letters with the initial "H," but they were written on the stationery of the U. S. Senate and the handwriting seems to have been that of Senator Henry Wilson, of Massachusetts. Senator Wilson, who later became Vice-President, was an important man for Rebel Rose to know in those early days of the war, for he was chairman of the Military Affairs Committee of the Senate—and so was privy to the most secret war plans.

The tone of one impassioned note suggests an affair of such ardor that the best-kept secrets were likely to escape from the lips of their supposed keeper.

"You well know that I love you—and will sacrifice anything," this flaming message began. "H" then discussed some mundane Senate affairs, including the Pacific Railroad bill in which, as was well-known, Senator Wilson was keenly interested at the time. Such less consequential matters disposed of, the enamored "H" reverted to the subject that was closest to his heart. "You know that I *do love* you," he wrote, with emphasis. "I am suffering this morning, in fact I am sick physically and mentally, and know that nothing could soothe me so much as an hour with you. And tonight, at whatever cost I will see you . . . I will be with you tonight, and then I will tell you again and again that I love you."

The red brick house at Thirteenth and I streets in which Rose now lived must have been the scene of many nighttime assignations. Though Senator Wilson may have thought he alone enjoyed the lady's favors, the record suggests otherwise. Years later, Colonel Thomas Jordan, a handsome West Pointer, disclosed that before he left Washington to join the Confederate Army he had learned of Rose's "intimacy" with Senator Wilson—and so he "had established relations with the widow on the same footing."

When duty ended Jordan's "relations" with Rose, he left her a cipher to use in sending him information she gathered about the movements of the Union Army. Rose promptly put the code to good use. When General Irvin McDowell started the advance that would lead to disaster at Bull Run, Rose kept Jordan informed step by step of exactly what McDowell intended to do before McDowell had a chance to do it.

She sent three messages south, on July 10, 16, and 17, 1861. The first was carried by a young black-haired and extremely beautiful Maryland girl, Betty Duvall, who dressed herself like a farmer's daughter and rode out of Washington in a farm cart. A small package no larger than a silver dollar, tied up in silk, was hidden under the "tucking comb" that kept her long raven locks in place. When she reached Confederate headquarters, she removed the comb and extracted the concealed message. It read: "McDowell has certainly been ordered to advance on the sixteenth. R.O.G."

In her second and most vital message, Rebel Rose informed the Confederates that McDowell "with 55,000 troops will advance this day [the sixteenth] from Arlington Heights." Though her troop figure was high, the rest of her information was uncannily accurate. It had to be because, as she later wrote, it came directly from McDowell's marching orders, which should have been top secret. With access to these, probably through Senator Wilson, Rebel Rose informed the Confederates that the Union Army would advance "to Manassas, via Fairfax Court House and Centreville."

No battlefield commander was ever blessed with more precise and accurate information about his enemy's movements and objectives. So favored, the Confederates set their trap at Manassas and routed McDowell—a victory so overwhelming that they were themselves astounded and failed to follow it up by marching into Washington, as it seems they could have done.

When McClellan took over command of the demoralized army, he soon discovered that Confederate spies infesting Washington were aware of his every move. There was little doubt in his mind about the major source of such leaks. Successful as Rebel Rose was, she had also been indiscreet. She had made no secret of her Southern sympathies. Everywhere she went in Washington social circles—and she still had contacts on the highest levels—she talked passionately about her devotion to the Southern cause. Worse still, she and the female collaborators in her espionage ring were so elated by the outcome of the Battle of Bull Run that, as one federal agent noted, they "openly boasted that the secret information given to the rebel generals had been mainly the cause of the defeat of our armies . . ."

Suspicion, therefore, focused almost instantly on Rose. She was still going her high-flying, gadabout way in social circles, getting the most secret information. She knew exactly what McClellan had said to Senator Wilson in the privacy of President Lincoln's own reception room in the White House. She knew the names of three new officers appointed to McClellan's staff before those names had been publicly announced. "She knew my plans," McClellan complained bitterly, "and four times has compelled me to change them."

Someone had to put an end to Rebel Rose's activities, and Allan Pinkerton was given the assignment. He gave orders "that a strict watch should be kept upon this house, and that every person entering or leaving the same should come under the close surveillance of my men."

Pinkerton called in several of his agents—Pryce Lewis, Sam Bridgeman, and John Scully among them—and set up watch over the Greenhow espionage nest, "a two-story brick and basement building, the parlors of which were elevated several feet above the ground . . ."

Surveillance should be conducted in such a manner that the suspect is unaware of being watched. But it seems evident that the Pinkerton men at the time were not very skilled in the art of unobtrusive tailing, for Rebel Rose soon became aware that she was being watched and followed everywhere she went.

She soon discovered, too, that the stocky, stoical, somewhat puritanical Allan Pinkerton was impervious to her most seductive smiles and dark-eyed come-hither glances. The wiles that had served her so well were now being scorned, and Rose reacted with catlike venom. She called Pinkerton "that German Jew detective" and referred to his agents as "ruffians" and "lawless men." She and her associated female spies, still not very discreet in behavior, sometimes even tried to play games with their "shadows," leading them on, concocting elaborate ways to elude them in the streets—their conduct making it perfectly clear that they knew what Pinkerton was doing, hardly a recommended procedure for a spy, who should always put forward the face of innocence.

This cat-and-mouse game came to an end one afternoon in early August, when Pinkerton decided to take more direct action. With two of his men, he set out to reconnoiter the home of Mrs. Greenhow. The day had been "dark, gloomy and threatening," and as Pinkerton left his office "a slight shower of rain was falling." After scouting the premises in person,

Pinkerton left two of his men on watch, returned to his head-quarters, and got three more agents for the night's activities.

It was dark by the time he got back to Rebel Rose's home, "and the rain fell in deluging torrents." Pinkerton found the venetian blinds on the lower windows closed, but light showed behind them in two rooms. The windows were too high from the ground for Pinkerton to have seen inside even if the blinds had not been closed; and so he took off his shoes, climbed up on the shoulders of two of his men, carefully pried up a sash, and turned the slats of the blind just enough to give him a full view of the room. It was empty.

There now began a jack-in-the-box farce. For the next few hours, Pinkerton spent a frustrating time hopping up and down from the ladderlike shoulders of his men for all the world like a child's puppet. He had hardly obtained his first peek into the empty parlor when it all began. One of his men hissed a warning "Sh!" Someone was approaching.

Pinkerton scrambled down and hid with his agents under the high stoop that led to the front door in the center of the house. The footsteps turned from the street and came up the walk; the visitor climbed the steps over Pinkerton's head and rang the bell.

As soon as the visitor had been admitted to the house, Pinkerton and his men hurried back to their positions under the jimmied window. The detective peeked through the blinds. There, sitting in Rebel Rose's parlor, he saw a captain in full uniform—a man "whom I had met that day for the first time." Pinkerton's description continues:

"He was a tall, handsome man of a commanding figure and about forty years of age. He had removed his cloak, and as he sat there in his blue uniform, and in the full glare of the gaslight, he looked a veritable ideal soldier. As I watched him closely, however, I noticed that there was a troubled, restless look upon his face; he appeared ill at ease and shifted nervously upon his chair, as though impatient for the entrance of his hostess. In a few moments Mrs. Greenhow entered and cordially greeted her visitor, who acknowledged her salutations with a courtly bow, while his face lighted up with pleasure as he gazed upon her."

Just at this crucial moment, when Pinkerton expected to learn much, another low-voiced warning came from his lookout. More steps were heard. Pinkerton jumped to the ground again; he and his men scurried to their hide-out under the porch steps—and waited there until the sound of footsteps died away in the stormy night.

Hopping up once more onto the sopping wet shoulders of his men, Pinkerton got another glance inside the parlor. Rose and the Union officer were sitting at a table in the rear of the room, talking in such low voices that Pinkerton could only catch a word here and there. But, as he watched, the officer drew "from an inner pocket of his coat a map which, as he held it up before the light, I imagined that I could identify as a plan of the fortifications in and around Washington." Pinkerton watched as the pair bent their heads close together over the map, pointing with their fingers to special points of interest.

Now once more came the warning signal from Pinkerton's lookout. More footsteps. Another scurry into the shelter of the stoop. Once more the footsteps faded away in the distance, and the impatient Pinkerton made another eager leap onto the shoulders of his long-suffering agents. But now he discovered, to his bitter disappointment, "the room was empty. The delectable couple had disappeared."

For more than an hour, while the storm raged and rain drummed upon his head, Pinkerton waited and watched and wondered what "the delectable couple" could be doing. Then "they re-entered the parlor, arm in arm, and again took their seats."

They had hardly done so when another warning came from the sidewalk. It seemed to be Pinkerton's misfortune on this inclement night that busybodies who didn't have the sense to stay at home came along the sidewalk just when Pinkerton most wanted to observe what was happening in Rose's parlor. There was no help for it, however. Once more, Pinkerton and his men had to scuttle to their refuge under the high front stoop. This time, as they waited there, Pinkerton heard the front door open "and the step of the traitor Captain above me. With a whispered good-night, and something that sounded very much like a kiss, he descended the steps . . ."

Pinkerton had now learned all that he was likely to learn. He knew the identity of the treacherous captain; and an experienced counterespionage agent would at this point probably have been content to let the man go, not wanting to arouse his suspicions, satisfied that his every movement could be watched in the future. But not Pinkerton.

Like Rose herself, Pinkerton was a bit of a novice at the spy game, and so he took off after the captain in his stocking feet. Because the night was so black and stormy, he had to tread dangerously close on his suspect's heels. The captain became aware that he was being followed. A couple of times he turned

his head, and Pinkerton saw him fingering his service revolver nervously. Still Pinkerton refused to give up the chase.

At the corner of Fifteenth Street and Pennsylvania Avenue,
the officer suddenly disappeared as if the night had swallowed
him. He had slipped into the doorway of a building before
which a sentry stood. Pinkerton had been so close on his heels
that he would have given himself away had he suddenly turned
tail in flight—and so he walked straight ahead into the arms of
four soldiers "who rushed suddenly upon me, with fixed bayonets pointed at my breast . . ." Almost before he knew what
was happening, the head of McClellan's secret service found
himself a prisoner.

What was even more humiliating, he was soon being grilled
by the very traitor he had been tracking. The Union captain
sat there, twirling a couple of revolvers, and demanded that
Pinkerton explain himself. Explanations were difficult. There
was Pinkerton, still in his stocking feet, mud-spattered, stream-
ing water, trying to pretend that he was just plain "E. J.
Allen," an innocent stroller in the stormy night. The captain
obviously didn't believe him, and Pinkerton found himself
thrown unceremoniously into an ice-cold cell with several
drunks, some common criminals, and two outspoken Southern
sympathizers.

In this fix, Pinkerton cultivated the acquaintance of a
sympathetic guard who brought him a blanket and who
promised that, as soon as he went off duty at 6 A.M., he
would take a note from Pinkerton to the Assistant Secretary
of War. The guard kept his promise; by 8:30 A.M. a squad of
soldiers arrived with orders from the War Department for
Pinkerton's release. It was clear, of course, that Pinkerton

must be a man of importance since the highest echelons of the department were concerned about his fate; and so the traitorous captain, who still had no inkling of what was involved, decided to accompany his prisoner to see what it was all about.

When the party arrived at the War Department, Assistant Secretary Thomas A. Scott realized that action had to be taken at once. He called the captain before him and questioned him about his activities of the previous night. The captain said he had been visiting "friends" on the outskirts of the city; on the way back, he had noticed that he was being followed—and so had ordered Pinkerton's arrest. Scott asked:

"Did you see anyone last evening who is inimical to the cause of the government?"

The captain denied any wrongdoing. Scott, increasingly grim, pressed him on the point again and again. The captain could only repeat his denial, but he was becoming obviously flustered. Scott then ordered him to hand over his sword and placed him under arrest.

In his account of this drama, Pinkerton later camouflaged the officer's identity, calling him "Captain Ellison." He appears to have been Captain John Elwood, of the Fifth Infantry, who had been appointed Provost Marshal of Washington on May 1, 1861. He was thrown into prison, but for some mysterious reason was released within a year. Pinkerton says only, "He died shortly afterward."

With the captain imprisoned, the question remained: What was to be done about Mrs. Greenhow? As Rebel Rose was unaware that her handsome captain had been arrested, it was decided to let her go her way and to keep a close watch on her movements in an effort to identify her other contacts. This watchfulness did, indeed, lead detectives to some other, lesser members of the Greenhow ring, but after several days it became clear that Rose was aware of the surveillance. Perhaps she felt apprehensive because she had not heard from the captain. Whatever the reason, she became more edgy and more bold, sometimes whipping around in the street to confront the Pinkerton men trailing her. Pinkerton decided that the time had come to end the game and to strike.

On the morning of August 23, Mrs. Greenhow went for a "promenade" with a man described only as "a diplomat." Whether he was in a position to pass her important information is not clear; but, according to her own subsequent account, by the time she returned from this diplomatic stroll, she had in her possession "a very important note." Aware that two Pinkerton agents had been following her, she paused on the sidewalk across the street from her home and inquired about the health of a neighbor's child who had been ill. Actually, this show of concern was only a pretext; the pause gave her an opportunity to study the situation on the street.

One of her own contacts sauntered casually past, whispering that her house had been under close surveillance and pointing to the two Pinkertons who were now standing a short distance away, up the street. Rose glared at them, and the Pinkerton men, aware she had spotted them, strolled past her "with an air of conscious authority." At the corner, they stopped and stared back at her, trading look for look.

Rose now had no doubt she was about to be arrested. Another of her spies passed by—the neighborhood seems to have been crawling with undercover agents of both sides—

53

and she murmured to him: "Those men will probably arrest me. Wait at Corcoran's Corner, and see. If I raise my handkerchief to my face, give information."

Her agent went off down the street, whistling nonchalantly. Rose slipped the "very important note" into her mouth, chewed—and swallowed. Then she crossed the road and started to climb the steps to the front door of her own house.

Instantly, Pinkerton in a major's uniform and one of his agents stepped up on either side of her.

"Is this Mrs. Greenhow?" Pinkerton asked.

"Yes."

There was a pause. Pinkerton and his agent were aware that they were dealing with a very highly placed lady; after all, in the last two weeks, they had seen a number of Congressmen coming to Rose's home, an indication that she still wielded powerful influence. Sensing their momentary hesitation, Rose demanded boldly: "Who are you and what do you want?"

"I come to arrest you," Pinkerton told her.

"By what authority?"

"By sufficient authority."

"Let me see your warrant."

Pinkerton had no warrant. He could only say that he was acting on oral instructions from both the State and War departments.

Rose, play-acting to the last, raised the handkerchief to her mouth and hoped that her watching agent would recognize the signal and warn the others in her ring. Then, with Pinkerton and his aide on either side of her, she permitted herself to be taken under guard into her own home. Still

54

haughty, she carried herself with the air of a woman who had power in Washington and despised these wormlike creatures who were presuming to arrest her.

"I have no power to resist you," she told Pinkerton. "But had I been inside my own house, I would have killed one of you before I had submitted to this illegal process."

"That would have been wrong," one of the detectives told her.

Pinkerton's men were now swarming all over the house.

"What are you going to do?" Rose demanded.

"To search," Pinkerton told her shortly.

Pinkerton called all his men inside the house, hoping to keep the arrest secret so that some of Rose's spying confederates might come calling and walk into the trap. This move was partly frustrated when Rose's little daughter slipped out, climbed a tree on the front lawn, and chanted: "Mother's been arrested! Mother's been arrested!" She continued to cry the alarm until the Pinkerton men pulled her down.

While this was going on, Pinkerton led his agents in ransacking Rose's lair. Boxes, bureau drawers, wastebaskets, books, scraps of paper from the fireplaces—all were combed for evidence, and there was a lot of it. Even though Rose had known she was under investigation (perhaps she thought nothing would come of it because of her high-level contacts), she had kept in her house a vast amount of incriminating evidence—the worst indiscretion a spy queen could possibly commit.

Pinkerton's search uncovered the secret cipher by which Rose had sent information to Jordan; the passionate love letters of Senator Wilson; a small red diary listing many of her couriers and fellow agents, some of them prominent Washingtonians; and copies of reports containing a mass of information about the movement of troops, the sizes and quantities of ordnance, and blueprints of the forts defending the capital.

In the midst of this search, Lily Mackell and her sister—two of the spies in Rose's ring—walked into the house. Rose had been arrested about 11 A.M., four hours earlier, and word had already reached Lily Mackell. But she was determined to find out what had happened to Rose and decided to take the risk of being arrested herself.

The instant she opened the door, according to Rose, a detective standing behind it shoved her and her sister "rudely" into the room. The two women fended off the detectives' questions and stayed with Rose the rest of the day.

Despite the vast amount of incriminating evidence Pinkerton had uncovered, Rose later insisted that he had missed the most important documents in her cache. According to the way she told the story, she waited until Pinkerton had left and then proceeded to use her wiles on his agents. The Greenhow cellar was well stocked with rum and brandy, and the Greenhow hospitality was famed for having on occasion mellowed the mood of Secretary of State Seward himself. The Pinkerton men were no match for this largess. They sampled the potions kind Rose put before them, and soon they were quarreling among themselves in voices loud enough to scare away any nocturnal visitors.

This was one of Rose's objectives, but she also had a second. When her guards were at their uncaring tipsiest, she slipped into her library, pulled a folio volume down from a high shelf, and hid it in her billowing dress. The volume, she later wrote, contained some of her most important papers, and she succeeded in smuggling these out of the house, concealed in Lily Mackell's shoes and garments, when the federal men escorted Lily and her sister to their own home between three and four o'clock the following morning.

Whatever the truth of this, the fact remained that Pinkerton had uncovered ample evidence about the far reach and importance of Rose's spy ring. Some of this evidence involved persons so highly placed that the Lincoln Administration was embarrassed and in a quandary about how to handle the explosive situation. A Cabinet meeting was called to discuss the problem; and Rose later wrote that Senator Wilson himself had been called to explain his actions. What explanation he gave was never recorded.

Pinkerton kept insisting that Rose must be jailed, but the administration ducked the issue for nearly five months. During that period, Rose was kept under guard in her home, which was referred to in the Washington press as "the Greenhow prison." It was not until January 18, 1862, that she was transferred to the Old Capitol Prison, a long three-story brick and wood building at East Capitol and Carroll streets.

Before she left her home for the last time, Rose toured it in the company of Pryce Lewis, to whom she denounced Pinkerton's "unwashed ruffians" for having left footprints on her rugs. A crowd had gathered in the street to see her leave—men and boys even climbed trees and lampposts to get a better look at her. She paused for a moment on the high steps and looked down, cold and contemptuous, at the sea of upturned faces. Then, putting on her most majestic air, she took her little daughter's hand and walked to the street. To the army lieutenant conducting her, she remarked sarcastically: "I hope in the future your men will have nobler employment."

Pinkerton himself had selected the room Rose was to have on the second floor of the prison. Old Capitol had formerly been the Old Congressional Boarding House; and, as chance would have it, the room Pinkerton chose for Rose was the very one in which, in an earlier day, she had sat by the bedside of the dying Senator Calhoun.

Even in prison, Rose was dangerous. She continued to see important callers, among them Senator Wilson. Her high-level friends in Washington—politicians, statesmen, and military leaders—exerted great pressure on the administration for her release. On one occasion, Assistant Secretary of the Navy Gustavus V. Fox called on Rose to tell her that she would be freed if she signed an oath of allegiance. Rose, of course, had no intention of doing any such thing; but, according to Pinkerton, she turned her "irresistible seductive powers" on Fox with such effect that she actually wormed out of him the secret plans for McClellan's next campaign. That same night—by what means was never known, for the fact itself wasn't discovered until Confederate archives were seized after the fall of Richmond—Rose smuggled out of Old Capitol and sent on the way to Jordan the detailed information she had gathered "from Fox of the Navy Department."

Pinkerton noted later that Rose, in prison, had suddenly become interested in making tapestries. She used balls of colored wool that were delivered to her through the provost marshal's office. The finished products, innocent enough in appearance, were sent out to her friends—and apparently contained the military information she was still gathering. She was permitted to write some letters, the authorities evidently hoping to catch her transmitting secret data; but Rose was too clever for them. She was using a new code provided for her by Jordan; and though the letters appeared to be innocent gibberish, they conveyed the messages she wished to send. Rose even flaunted her success in the administration's face. She smuggled out a long letter to the Richmond *Whit*. When the newspaper published it in full, it created a sensation. It described how Pinkerton's "ruffians" had "torn letters from my bosom," and the fact that this wasn't true didn't lessen the embarrassment of Lincoln and his Cabinet.

While tempestuous Rose was proving herself too much of a handful for her jailers, Pinkerton was doggedly tracking down members of her spy ring. Following leads he had obtained in searching Rose's home, the detective made arrest after arrest. He never captured all of Rose's agents, but he arrested several of the more prominent ones.

One of those captured was William J. Walker, a clerk in the Post Office Department, who had a direct link to Jordan; another was Michael Thompson, a polished and suave South Carolina lawyer, whose home yielded a raft of dispatches and reports destined for Richmond, including a copy of the Jordan cipher that had been used by Rose. The arrest of Thompson, known to the Confederates by the code name of "Colonel Empty," led to another important espionage agent, William T. Smithson, a prominent Washington banker and a close friend of Rose. Smithson, Pinkerton learned, had devised a novel means of getting information to Richmond, rolling his messages up tightly and concealing them in plugs of tobacco.

Despite Pinkerton's ceaseless activity, Rose Greenhow, with her ability to spy from behind prison bars, became too dangerous a prisoner to keep. Since it was not the custom to execute women spies in those more chivalrous days, the Lincoln Administration finally decided to get rid of her. And so, in early June 1962, Rebel Rose was taken to Fortress Monroe, where she signed a promise "not to return north of the Potomac during the present hostilities without the permission of the Secretary of War of the U.S." With this, she was released and sent on to the Rebel capital in Richmond.

The strain of the long months in prison had left its mark on her. Her hair was streaked with gray, her fabled beauty collapsing into wrinkled age. Jefferson Davis, who had known her in happier times, wrote his wife on June 13: "Madam looks much changed, and has the air of one whose nerves have been shaken by mental torture."

She was still, however, Rebel Rose—the passionate believer in the Confederate cause. And she was determined to get even with Allan Pinkerton, the detective whom she blamed for her downfall. With the manuscript of a book she had finished, describing her experiences, she sailed on a blockade runner for England. There her book was a sensation and made her the heroine of the hour. On her return trip, the blockade runner carrying her grounded on a shoal while trying to run into Wilmington, N.C., and Rebel Rose tried to reach shore in a small boat. The boat capsized in heavy seas, and she was drowned.

7
Union
Spy Master

ALLAN PINKERTON was not only a successful hunter of Southern spies; he was the master of a far-flung spy network of his own. In the first role, he scored notable successes; in the second, he was in many respects a failure.

It was not that the daring agents he sent into the South did not gather excellent information. They did. The trouble lay with Pinkerton himself. An excellent detective, he lacked the training necessary for a military intelligence chief. Not a military man, he had difficulty assessing the value of the voluminous reports that poured in upon him from all directions. And so, unfortunately, he had a tendency to see two Confederates where there was only one.

The most daring and successful of Pinkerton's spies, up to a point, was Timothy Webster. This powerfully built, bearded agent had infiltrated the secessionist groups around Baltimore in the early and successful effort to protect Lincoln's life, and

Pinkerton sent him back to the area when Baltimore erupted in the kind of rebellion he had predicted.

On April 19, 1861, the Maryland city exploded in violence. The Sixth Massachusetts Regiment, on its way from the north to reinforce the slender squads in the almost defenseless capital, had to pass through Baltimore. There mobs of Southern sympathizers assailed the troops, hurling rocks, firing rifles. Colonel Elmer E. Ellsworth and three of his men were killed, and thirty-one were wounded. The soldiers had to fight their way through the Baltimore streets to board the train that brought them to Washington, dirty, haggard, and exhausted.

After the troops had escaped their clutches, the Baltimore rioters went on a binge of destruction. Railroad bridges were destroyed, severing rail communication with Washington, and the telegraph lines were cut. For a time, the capital on the Potomac was all but cut off, facing a hostile Virginia on the south, with a rebellious Maryland menacing its other boundaries.

The Maryland uprising was ultimately quelled, but Baltimore remained a hotbed, ripe for another outbreak at any moment. To keep tabs on the situation, Pinkerton sent Timothy Webster and Hattie Lawton back to Perrymansville to renew acquaintance with their former contacts. John Scully acted as their courier.

Webster was so successful that he became a member of the Knights of Liberty, a Confederate fifth column. A persuasive and powerful speaker, Webster soon worked himself into a position of leadership in the Knights and became a courier for them, carrying secret dispatches to Confederate Secretary of War Judah P. Benjamin in Richmond.

By this activity, Webster learned the details of a co-ordinated plan by which the South hoped to seize Washington. At a given signal from Richmond, timed to coincide with an attack by the Confederate Army from the south, some ten thousand Baltimoreans would rise and take over the city. Webster thought that the Knights exaggerated the number of their followers, but he reported to Pinkerton that they did, indeed, have a quantity of rifles. He had seen them.

Acting on Webster's information, Pinkerton arranged with McClellan and the Secretary of War for a raid on an important meeting of the leaders of the Knights. The meeting hall was quietly ringed with troops, and at a given signal the doors were smashed in and the Knights were caught in their seats with their hands down.

Pinkerton took care, in directing the raid, not to blow Webster's cover. He waited until another of his undercover agents had signaled that Webster was in the middle of a fiery speech, denouncing Lincoln and the Union. Webster's reaction when the doors burst open and troops flooded the hall must have seemed, therefore, only natural. He turned and leaped out a rear window like a man in full flight from the hated enemy.

With his Southern credentials still intact, Webster "fled" to Richmond, where he set up headquarters in the Spotswood Hotel and became a daily visitor to Secretary Benjamin's office. He was so trusted by Benjamin that he was soon carrying the most secret dispatches and even personal messages sent by the Secretary. And at night, surrounded by enemies, facing the possibility of exposure at any instant, he prepared for

Allan Pinkerton the most meticulous, detailed reports, many of them pages long.

This most remarkable spy career finally was interrupted by illness. Webster was confined to his hotel room with inflammatory rheumatism, and Pinkerton sent Hattie Lawton to Richmond to nurse him. Since he also needed someone to bring Webster's information north, he decided to send Pryce Lewis and John Scully to make contact with Webster and Hattie Lawton. Lewis, who had had his fill of espionage in West Virginia, protested against going and against taking Scully with him. One agent, he argued, might get his cover story down pat, but with two there was always the danger that one would slip up on details and expose them both. Pinkerton argued him out of both positions, and Lewis and Scully went to Richmond. Disaster followed.

Shortly after their arrival, the Pinkerton agents visited Webster in his hotel room. While they were there, one of Webster's highly placed Confederate friends came to inquire about his health. Unfortunately, the man had with him the young son of former Senator Jackson Morton, whom Lewis and Scully had guarded when the Morton family was arrested during Pinkerton's roundup of Confederate spies in Washington. Young Morton recognized the pair as Pinkerton's men; exposure and arrest followed.

Pinkerton, it later developed, had protested against the release of Mrs. Greenhow and the other Southern spies held in Washington as long as his agents were in Richmond, but his protest had been ignored by the War Department. And now his spies in Richmond paid the price.

Scully's nerves became unraveled when he was faced with

the specter of the gallows. He broke and confessed all, dooming Timothy Webster. This gallant spy, already wasted away to a shadow of his once robust self by his illness, was executed. Hattie Lawton, Scully, and Lewis were imprisoned but ultimately released.

While this tragic drama was being played out in Richmond, Pinkerton himself had taken the field with McClellan's Army of the Potomac. As McClellan's eyes and ears, "Major E. J. Allen" pitched his tent by the side of his commander's. The association was close and, on the whole, unfortunate. Pinkerton revered McClellan, but his own flaws as an intelligence chief reacted on the worst weakness of his commander.

McClellan was, in many respects, a brilliant general. He was a genius as an organizer and a sound strategist. He had taken the rabble that fled from Bull Run and welded it into an effective fighting force. He was worshiped by his men. But he lacked one vital quality: a soldier is supposed to fight, and McClellan was no fighter. He was supercautious, his imagination always picturing double the number of bayonets that were actually arrayed against him, always creating for him difficulties and hazards that did not exist. For such a man, Allan Pinkerton was the worst possible intelligence chief.

Pinkerton's analyses were not always wrong. Indeed, at times they were almost brilliant. His agents behind enemy lines sent him detailed information on almost everything—from the supplies of coffee, lead, salt, and camp kettles to reports on the strength of individual Confederate units, the construction of fortifications, and the field of fire of their guns. From this mass of data, Pinkerton deduced in November 1861 that the Confederates had 117,100 armed men in the field. After the war, official records of the Confederacy showed that there had actually been 118,306.

For every such on-the-mark assessment, however, Pinkerton came up with two or three that were so exaggerated as to be ludicrous. One source of error seems to have been his reliance on the word of escaping black slaves. The old-time abolitionist in him, his long sympathy for the plight of the blacks, warped his judgment. In the field with McClellan, he would question escaping blacks as they came into camp, and he appears to have made little allowance for the obvious: that these were ignorant and untrained refugees whose frightened minds magnified everything they had seen. To them, Southern forces appeared to be a veritable host—and Pinkerton believed them.

Even years later, after the war, Pinkerton kept insisting that Confederate forces opposing McClellan before Richmond in 1862 had numbered some 200,000 men. Actually, as Confederate records showed, they totaled a mere 86,000—and McClellan had had more than 100,000 under his own direct command, with 100,000 guarding Washington.

It would have been better for the Union cause if Pinkerton's tendency had been to underestimate by one half instead of overestimating by 100 per cent. As it was, McClellan's natural timidity received support and confirmation from Pinkerton's supposedly reliable figures, and the dashing Little Mac fought on the defensive when he should have lashed out and routed an inferior foe.

Lincoln, in time, got tired of McClellan's faulty judgment and removed him from command of the army. Pinkerton was convinced that this was the work of some evil "Washington cabal" out to discredit his favorite general—and so he resigned on November 7, 1862, as head of the army's secret service. He spent the rest of the war in minor tasks, investigating frauds against the government, the kind of detective work in which he was most expert.

He was in New Orleans when the war ended, and it was there that he received the word, flashed over the telegraph wires, that Lincoln had been assassinated in Ford's Theatre in Washington. Pinkerton's son William later recalled how his father crumpled the message in his hands and wept.

"If I had only been there to protect him as I was before," he murmured.

8
Tracking
Desperadoes

THE PERIOD immediately follow-
ing the Civil War was probably the most lawless in American
history. It was a time for rogues, high and low. The upper
stratum of American life was riddled with corruption as Wall
Street manipulators watered stocks, bought influence, created
panics—and all but brought the country to ruin. Hard times
produced desperate men.

When the war ended, some million and a half soldiers were
thrown on a labor market already glutted. The war had taught
these veterans how to hunt and kill, and many used their lethal
skills in lawless raids on the rich sources of booty created by
the nation's rapidly expanding industrial economy.

Railroads now threaded the nation from coast to coast,
passing through wide-open spaces where there was no law
worthy of the name. The idea of a Federal Bureau of Investigation had not yet been born. There was no central bureau

keeping a file on criminals and their records. There was only the Pinkerton agency.

The Pinkertons in this lawless period filled a role similar to the one assumed some sixty years later by J. Edgar Hoover and the FBI. The agency's business expanded on a broad front as railroads, express carriers, banks, and other institutions appealed for protection against the criminal hordes. To meet the demand, Allan Pinkerton opened a New York office in 1866 to handle cases in the eastern and southern states. His sons, William and Robert, had finished schooling at Notre Dame and had joined him in the agency. Robert was sent east to head the New York office, with the veteran George Bangs as superintendent. William commanded the Chicago headquarters. But titles in this era did not mean much; there was only one real Pinkerton boss—the driving, tireless, increasingly tyrannical Allan Pinkerton.

Every detail of every case, no matter how insignificant, had to be forwarded to Chicago for his personal examination. The founder's fanatic insistence that he must check everything imposed upon him an impossible, superhuman burden. It took its toll in overwork and increasing tension. Like a drowning man furiously thrashing water, Allan Pinkerton lashed about him, trying futilely to cope with the flood of detail that poured down upon him, taking out his frustration in angry, carping letters to George Bangs and Robert. Even Allan's iron constitution began to rebel against the strains imposed upon it, and he had to pause at times in the midst of dictating a letter, wincing at the severe, blinding headaches that seemed to strike out of the blue—warning signals that he refused to heed.

This was the man who now fought—with every furious

and energetic fiber of his being—the terror that stalked the states of the Middle Border.

Jesse James and his band of cutthroats have gone down in folklore as epitomizing this era of train holdups, banditry, and lawlessness that terrorized entire communities. But in the annals of the Pinkertons, James and his gang were eclipsed by a band that attracted less national notoriety—but actually raided more, stole more, terrorized more. These were the Reno brothers of Indiana.

The Renos came from Jefferson County in the rural, southern portion of the state. Wilkinson Reno, the father of the outlaws, was an illiterate who, one of his sons said later, "could hardly count his own money"; but the record says he possessed a certain low-down cunning about how money was to be made. Parcel by parcel, he acquired a large tract of farmland until he became one of the largest property owners in the county.

Wilkinson's outlaw sons were born in the late 1830s and early 40s. Frank, the oldest, was born on the family farm near Seymour—the town that the Reno outlaws were virtually to appropriate as their own, in the tradition later emphasized by Wild West movies. The original leader of the band was the second son, John, born in 1839. Two younger sons, William and Simeon, rode stirrup by stirrup with Frank and John.

As a boy, John Reno was athletic, vigorous, with a talent for leadership. He attended a log-cabin school that his father had built on his Seymour farm; but, as he later wrote, he would sit for an hour with a book propped up in front of him, never seeing a word. In 1855, when he was sixteen, he ran away from home and wandered for a year through the South, working on plantations and learning the ways of life from riverboat gamblers.

Shortly after his return to Seymour, a strange disaster hit the countryside. Fire after fire broke out in the neighboring town of Rockford. Houses, churches, a newspaper plant, packing houses—all went up in flames. Residents fled from the blackened, gutted town into Seymour—and then the Renos purchased the ruins for $600.95!

A Reno relative was arrested on a charge of arson, found guilty—and fined fifty cents! An angry countryside began to talk of lynching, and Wilkinson Reno decided to move his family to St. Louis. By 1860, however, the fury of the moment having passed, he and his troublesome brood returned to Seymour.

With the outbreak of the Civil War, the Reno boys all became patriots, at least temporarily. They enlisted in the Union forces, and John Reno later described how he had taken part in the battle of Rich Mountain in West Virginia, "storming the breastworks with twenty-five of us behind our colonel." By 1863, however, all of the Renos had deserted and John had been arrested for stealing his captain's wallet.

Seymour at war's end became a veritable capital of crime. Confidence men swindled returning veterans of their pay checks; those who objected were beaten and murdered. Armed bands of robbers roamed the countryside, raping, pillaging, murdering. It was a lawless world, perfectly suited to the appetites of John Reno and his scoundrelly brothers, and they soon asserted their leadership over all the bandits and crooks in the area.

From the fall of 1865 to the fall of 1866, the Reno gang

robbed and stole with impunity. They even raided the Clinton County, Indiana, treasury; and though Frank Reno was arrested for the crime, he was promptly acquitted.

Then, on October 6, 1866, the Renos pulled the caper that, ultimately, after a long and hard chase, was to be their undoing. They committed what is said to have been the first formal train holdup in the United States—a deed that put Allan Pinkerton on their trail.

As an Ohio and Mississippi Railroad train pulled out of the Seymour station on that October day, three masked men boarded it. They were John and Simeon Reno and one of the Renos' principal henchmen, their favorite horse-holder, Franklin Sparks. The bandits slugged the Adams Express Company guard into unconsciousness, entered the baggage compartment, and seized two Adams safes. Three miles east of the town, at a lonely country spot where confederates were waiting, they shoved the safes off the train.

The smaller safe, which the robbers cracked open on the spot, contained $15,000. The larger and stronger safe had $30,000 in cash and gold, but the robbers, unable to open it, finally abandoned it by the roadside.

Since Adams Express had been one of Allan Pinkerton's oldest and most important accounts, he hurried at once to Indiana to investigate the holdup in person. He soon found that the Reno gang was running roughshod over decent citizens and that they dominated the whole county by their brutality, the fear they inspired—and bribery.

Pinkerton had one favorite tactic in cases of this kind. He called it "laying pipe with the outlaws"—in other words, infiltrating the gang.

The exact technique that he used to accomplish this in the Reno case is not clear. It is known that, by some means, he persuaded the owner of a new saloon in Seymour—a man known as Dick Winscott—to play an undercover role for him. With Winscott secretly working for the Pinkertons, several of the agency's best detectives drifted in and made the dingy, smoky saloon their headquarters.

No actor ever played a role better than Winscott. He let it be known that he had been involved in some skulduggery back East; and the Renos, sensing a kindred spirit, let their guard down in his tavern. They lounged at the tables, drank at the rough bar, played games with their women—and discussed plans for their next forays just as if no ears were listening. During one carousal, Winscott even managed to persuade John Reno and Sparks to climb up on stools and pose for a photographer, beer glasses in hand, drunken leers on their faces. Unknown to the Renos, the photographic print was soon on its way to Chicago, there to become an invaluable bit of evidence in Pinkerton's rogues' gallery.

The Renos' success inevitably inspired imitators. Two brash young cutthroats soon decided to copy their tactics. Boarding a train near Seymour, they robbed the Adams Express car of $8,000. The Renos were almost as incensed as Pinkerton. They were enraged that others had the nerve to infringe on their train-robbery patent—and on their own turf at that. And they had a second grievance: one of the brash young robbers had been courting John Reno's "fast woman."

With professional and amorous jealousies aroused, the Renos formed their own posse and took out after the train robbers. They caught them, thrashed them, hijacked the $8,000

—and then, acting for all the world like good citizens helping the law, they turned the brash rogues who had offered them a double insult over to the sheriff of Jackson County for prosecution.

The gang's next deed was more in character. They descended upon the Daviess County Treasury in Gallatin, Missouri, and made off with $22,065.

Though Pinkerton had no contract to protect the Daviess County Treasury, his friends in Adams Express asked him to investigate the case. Here the photograph Winscott had obtained of John Reno and Sparks proved helpful: it enabled witnesses to identify the Reno gang as the robbers.

But one thorny problem remained: how to make an arrest? Pinkerton conferred with Winscott and his other undercover men in Seymour. All assured him that if the Pinkertons rode into town and tried to arrest the Renos, there would be a pitched battle in which innocent persons would probably be caught in the cross fire and slain.

Allan and William Pinkerton mulled over the problem in their Chicago office. They decided there was only one solution. They would have to kidnap John Reno right from the midst of his followers. William Pinkerton contended later it was the only way and "the ends justified the means."

Allan Pinkerton wired the sheriff of Daviess County to meet him in Cincinnati with a warrant for John Reno's arrest. Then he sent Winscott a coded message. It instructed Winscott to lure Reno to the Seymour railroad depot, then to let Pinkerton know the exact day and hour the unsuspecting Reno would be set up for the snatch.

In Cincinnati, Pinkerton, with his railroad contacts, had no difficulty in hiring a special train. He rounded up six bruisers to help him, then waited for two days, the wood-burning locomotive at the ready, until the anticipated wire arrived from Winscott. It informed Pinkerton of the exact hour that John Reno would be standing on the station platform, "waiting for a friend" due to arrive on the express from Cincinnati.

Pinkerton's special train took off down the tracks ahead of the express and chugged into the Seymour depot just minutes ahead of the expected train. Looking out the window, Pinkerton saw Winscott on the platform laughing and talking with a burly, black-haired man wearing a rumpled blue suit and a crushed black hat. Pinkerton took one glance at the photograph he had brought along from his rogues' gallery and told his kidnapers: "That's our man."

The wheels of the train were still turning when Pinkerton swung down on the station platform, followed by his men. Since the arrival of a train was a town event in those days, a considerable crowd had gathered, waiting for the express. No one paid much attention to Pinkerton and his assistants as they sifted through the throng until they ringed John Reno. Only at the last second did Reno become aware of what was happening, and then he lunged wildly, like a rat caught in a trap, trying to break free. Pinkerton's bully boys quickly overpowered him, pinioned his arms behind him, and carried him, kicking and screaming for help, aboard the waiting train. Pinkerton, the last man aboard, waved his hand to the engineer, and the train huffed and puffed out of the station, leaving an amazed and gaping crowd on the platform.

Word of the daring kidnaping of the leader spread like a prairie fire through Seymour, and John Reno's followers mounted and rode furiously to the rescue. They soon discovered, however, that the speed of their horses was no match for the speed of Pinkerton's special train. Frustrated and furious, they returned to Seymour while Pinkerton lodged John Reno in the Gallatin jail. On the morning of January 18, 1868, the bandit leader, having pleaded guilty and been given a twenty-five year term, was transferred under heavy guard to the Missouri State Penitentiary at Jefferson City. Though he could not appreciate it at the time, this was the most fortunate thing that could have happened to John Reno.

Frank Reno now became the leader of the gang. Simeon and William Reno, together with Franklin Sparks, invariably rode with him. In defiance of the Pinkertons and the law, the gang now slashed its brutal way across the Middle Border states, raiding county treasuries, post offices, trains. In February 1868 they hit the Harrison County Treasury in Magnolia, Iowa, and made off with $14,000. The county supervisors asked Pinkerton to investigate.

Allan sent his oldest son, William, twenty-two, to Iowa. William was a stocky, powerfully built, younger edition of his father. He also had inherited Allan Pinkerton's dogged determination. In Iowa he spent long, monotonous days, questioning townsfolk, farmers, travelers; and he finally discovered that the bandits had fled from the scene of the robbery on a railroad handcar which they had abandoned some seven miles out of town.

William Pinkerton then concentrated on the countryside near the spot where the handcar had been discarded. He stopped at every farmhouse, questioned everyone he met—a laborious procedure that seemed for a time to yield little useful information. Bit by bit, however, William Pinkerton pieced together slender clues and traced the gang to Council Bluffs, Iowa. He reasoned that the Renos of Seymour, Indiana, strangers in the area, must have some old home-town contact that had drawn them to Council Bluffs; and he instructed his detectives to find out if there was a "disreputable place" in the neighborhood owned by a former resident of Seymour.

His hunch was good. A former Seymour counterfeiter was now running a Council Bluffs saloon. William Pinkerton ordered his men to keep a day-and-night watch on the place. Before long, this surveillance paid off, producing a significant bit of information. A regular visitor to the saloon was Michael Rogers, one of the wealthiest men in Council Bluffs and a pillar of the Methodist Church. Pinkerton sent a coded message to the head office in Chicago and got back the word that Rogers, the model citizen and churchman, had an old police record.

Suspicion mounting, William Pinkerton next traced Rogers' movements on the day of the raid on the county treasury in Magnolia. He learned that Rogers had paid his taxes at the office shortly before it closed, and he theorized that Rogers had cased the place and tipped off the Renos.

The next move was to keep Rogers' home under close surveillance. A dark-skinned man answering Frank Reno's description was seen visiting the house. The following day, just before dawn, Frank Reno led three other men to the back door, and they slipped inside. Pinkerton knew that the gang must be up to something, and it wasn't long before he learned what it was: the safe in the office of the Mills County Treasury had been cracked and $12,000 stolen.

William Pinkerton decided it was time to act. But, as he later recalled, when he asked local authorities for a warrant, they "laughed in my face at the thought of Mr. Rogers being implicated." Pinkerton had to convince them. He demonstrated that the same *modus operandi* had been used in both the Mills County and Magnolia raids: in each case the gang had escaped by using a railroad handcar which they had abandoned at an isolated rendezvous point. Pinkerton showed the second abandoned handcar to the sheriff, who, still only half-convinced, reluctantly issued a search warrant for the raid on Rogers' home.

Quietly surrounding the house in the predawn darkness, William Pinkerton and his men waited for the first streaks of light before leading the assault. He crashed in the front door at the head of his raiders and found Frank Reno eating breakfast with Albert Perkins and Miles Ogle, two top counterfeiters. Reno leaped to his feet, cursing and threatening to sue the Pinkertons.

Leaving one man to cover the three at gunpoint, Pinkerton led the search of the house. He found two sets of burglars' tools, but nothing else—none of the loot for which he was searching. Returning to the kitchen, he caught a faint whiff of smoke and noticed a fine wisp curling up from under a lid of the big iron stove. Yanking off the lid, Pinkerton found the $14,000 in bills taken from the Magnolia safe. The money was just beginning to crisp and smolder on the coals. Apparently, the gang had managed to distract the attention of the Pinkerton guard just long enough for one of them to slip the incriminating loot into the coal range in the hope of destroying the evidence.

Pinkerton arrested Frank Reno, Rogers, Ogle, and Perkins. They were packed away in the Council Bluffs jail in lieu of bail—but not for long. Just twenty-four hours later, Pinkerton got word that the four had "broken out" and escaped. Chalked in large letters above a hole that the supposedly weaponless bandits had mysteriously punched into the solid brick and mortar of the wall were the words: APRIL FOOL. It was April 1, 1868.

The Renos were on the loose again, free to raid and terrorize the Middle Border, and just a little more than a month later they pulled off their greatest coup—the holdup of the Marshfield Express.

This Ohio and Mississippi Valley train left Jeffersonville, Indiana, on the night of May 22, 1868. At 11 P.M. the express stopped to take on wood and water at Marshfield, then a fueling station about fourteen miles south of Seymour. Here a band of outlaws appeared suddenly out of the night and leaped aboard the stopped train.

They knocked out David Hutchinson, the fireman, and clubbed George Fletcher, the engineer, into unconsciousness. The bandits next uncoupled the locomotive, tender, and express cars from the rest of the train. One of the gang, John J. Moore, "a desperate outlaw" noted for having previously stolen a locomotive in making his getaway from the scene of a crime, was at the throttle and started the wood-burner down the tracks. Americus Wheeler, the conductor, fired a shot at the escaping gang, but was felled, seriously wounded, by a return volley of bullets.

As the hijacked section of the train chugged into the night, Frank Reno and his followers crawled over the top of the baggage car and dropped down to the car's platform. They smashed open the door and overwhelmed the Adams Express Company messenger. They beat the man almost to death, then hurled his unconscious body out of the car. He was found by the side of the tracks the next morning, barely alive.

Inside the baggage car, the bandits forced open iron safes that were four feet long and two feet wide. Out tumbled the richest haul the Renos had seized in their violent career—$96,000 in cash and government bonds. The loot was crammed into sacks; and at an isolated spot in the countryside, where Sparks was waiting with horses, the locomotive was abandoned.

The gang split up, its members seeking safety in different refuges. Five—Frank Reno, Charlie Anderson, Albert Perkins, Michael Rogers, and Miles Ogle—fled to Canada. Simeon and William Reno hid out with friends in Indianapolis. Sparks, Moore, and Henry Jerrell, a housepainter who, Pinkerton thought, "had been led astray" by the Renos, ducked into Coles County, Illinois, some twenty-seven miles west of Terre Haute, Indiana.

The first break came when Moore, carried away by the easy success of the Marshfield Express job, decided to lead a second foray, using the Renos' copyright. The flaw in his plan was that he couldn't organize such a raid as craftily as the Renos.

Moore made the mistake of propositioning a train engineer, George Flanders, to tip off the gang when his train was carrying its next big shipment of money. Flanders, an honest man, contacted Pinkerton. The great detective instantly saw and seized his opportunity. He instructed Flanders to play along with the gang and to tell them that his train was going to be carrying $100,000 in cash. When Flanders relayed this information to Moore, the bandit's greedy eyes lighted up, and he kept repeating over and over, in a marveling tone, "That is a lot of money."

Moore's gang for this second raid included, besides himself, Franklin Sparks, the veteran Reno horse-holder; Fril Clifton, who had cased many jobs for the Renos; Val Elliott, "a dashing and romantic looking man who had once been a brakeman" on the railroad; Charlie Roseberry, a former captain in the Union Army who had turned outlaw; and Jerrell, the housepainter who had been led astray.

The holdup took place on the night of July 10, 1868, near Shields, a small fueling station for wood and water about six miles west of Seymour. It seemed to go off without a hitch. Moore, gun in hand, climbed into the cab and "trussed up" Flanders, his supposed accomplice. The engine and express car were unhitched from the rest of the train, just as in the Marshfield caper, and Moore, at the throttle, went down the tracks to an isolated spot two miles outside of Brownstown.

Here the hijacked train was stopped, and Moore's gang jimmied the door of the express car and began to climb in. Inside, unknown to them, a squad of Pinkertons was waiting.

A wild scene now took place in the dark express car. Guns began to go off like a whole row of firecrackers exploding at once. Flying bullets filled the air as the hostile forces blazed away at each other. The Pinkertons, crouching low and having the advantage of surprise, were not touched, but Moore was shot four times, Jerrel suffered a fractured kneecap, and Elliott was struck in one shoulder.

"Run, run—it's all up with us," Moore shouted as he leaped from the car and fled the battle scene.

Roseberry, Clifton, and Sparks, who were *not* wounded, tried to cover the flight of their crippled comrades by firing a barrage at the Pinkertons. The train engineer, Flanders, having freed himself from Moore's loosely tied bonds, now took a hand in the fight. He shot off one of Sparks's fingers, but Moore fired back and brought down Flanders with a shattered knee.

Elliott, weak from loss of blood, surrendered to the Pinkertons, who carried him with them on the train to Brownstown. A few hours later, Roseberry and Clifton were captured in a thicket near the ghost village of Rockford.

The entire countryside was now aroused. The depredations of the Renos had spawned a vigilante moment, violence in the cause of justice vying with the violence of the lawless. Even Seymour, so long the fief of the Renos, was now divided into two armed camps, vigilantes against outlaws; and much evidence indicates that train crews—so long victimized, so savagely beaten and manhandled—had begun to work hand in glove with the vigilantes.

The result was lynching. On July 20, the Pinkertons and a number of Jackson County deputies attempted to move their prisoners from Cincinnati to Brownstown for arraignment on robbery charges. At a point about three miles out of Seymour, a number of lights flashed on the track ahead. The engineer, who claimed afterward that he was afraid he might be crashing his train into the rear of a freight, threw on the brakes. As the train jolted to a stop, more than two hundred night riders, their faces hidden behind scarlet flannel masks, swarmed around. The leader told the Pinkertons and deputies to get lost.

Unable to fight such a mob, the detectives heeded his advice. The vigilantes dragged the three prisoners—Roseberry, Clifton, and Elliott—from the train. Three ropes were thrown over the stout branch of a huge beech tree near a spot that was to be forever known as Hangman's Crossing, and the three train robbers were jerked aloft to strangling, contorted death. The grim deed took only five minutes, and it was performed "so quietly that a German farmer living but a few rods away from the hanging tree was not aroused." He woke in the morning to the shock of finding three bodies dangling from the tree limb almost at his front door.

Moore, Sparks, and Jerrell were still at large, but the Pinkertons were on their trail. Here, as was so often the case, Allan Pinkerton's attention to minute details, his careful amassing of complete dossiers in the Chicago headquarters, provided the vital clue. Through the agency's exhaustive researches on every individual member of the gang, Pinkerton had learned that Jerrell had a girl friend in Louisville, Kentucky. He ordered a watch kept on her home. Soon a postman was seen delivering a letter. The watching Pinkerton agent who learned that the girl couldn't read, arranged with a kindly neighbor to let the girl—and him—know what the letter said. It was signed "George Hudson," an alias Jerrell used, and it informed the girl friend that he was hiding out on a farm in Aetna, Illinois.

The Pinkertons swarmed into Aetna and arrested Moore, Jerrel, and Sparks. They took the bandit trio to Indianapolis, where they were jailed overnight. Late the next day, they were put on a train to take them to Brownstown for arraignment. Ironically, they were confined in the same bullet-pocked express car in which the gun battle with the Pinkertons had taken place.

The schedule called for the Ohio and Mississippi train to reach Seymour in time to transfer the prisoners to a 9 P.M. westbound train for Brownstown. But the train bearing the Pinkertons, sheriff's deputies, and the prisoners encountered some of the most mysterious delays in the history of railroading. It kept stopping every few miles with the engineer hopping out and examining the wheels as if he wanted to assure himself they still were round. Stops at station platforms became longer and longer. The Pinkerton guards, sensing that something was wrong, questioned the train crew—but got no satisfactory answers.

These delaying tactics dumped the Pinkertons and their prisoners at the Seymour station at 10:30 P.M., long after the connecting train had departed. The Pinkertons, in the heart of Reno territory, hired a horse and wagon in the hope of smuggling their prisoners into Brownstown.

They had gone only about three miles from Seymour when a horde of night riders, hundreds strong, charged out of the forest and surrounded the wagon. One detective aimed his rifle at the mob, but a vigilante knocked up his gun and beat him into unconsciousness. The Pinkertons and deputies were swiftly overwhelmed and told to "trot for Seymour and don't look back." Having no choice, they followed the advice.

The vigilantes drove the wagon containing the prisoners under the same Hangman's Crossing beech tree used in the previous lynching. Nooses were put around the necks of

Moore, Sparks, and Jerrell; the wagon was driven out from under them; and, the next morning, the German farmer was startled to find three more corpses swinging from his tree limb.

These lynchings fanned the flames of passion in the countryside. Vigilantes, thirsting for more blood, threatened to hang the Reno brothers out of hand if they could find them, and Reno henchmen retaliated by threatening vengeance on the vigilantes and anyone who helped them. Tempers flared at the wake for the lynched men. A sister of Moore's knocked a suspected vigilante down a flight of stairs, calling him, "a dirty Jew." Rising and brushing himself off, the man shouted at the screaming woman: "Madam, you are only a hussy and should have been hanged up with your damned brother."

In this atmosphere of increasing hatred and violence, a Pinkerton sleuth ran William and Simeon Reno to earth in southern Indiana on July 22. Then the battle began to keep them out of the vigilantes' hands until they could be tried for their crimes. The Pinkertons spirited the brothers from jail to jail under heavy guard, until they finally got them to the lockup in Lexington, eighteen miles north of Madison, Indiana. The sheriff appealed to the governor for help, and a detachment of state militia was sent into the town.

Only the presence of the militia kept the vigilantes from charging full tilt into Lexington to seize the Renos. On July 30, the brothers, dressed in black and wearing broad-brimmed black hats, were marched into court for arraignment. The courtroom was mobbed. When the Renos pleaded, "Not guilty," a riot broke out.

Men leaped over benches and tried to reach the Renos. They fought with the militia who struggled to beat them back

86

with rifle butts. Shouts, screams, and curses filled the air. Judge P. H. Jewett pounded for order with his gavel and called to the soldiers: "Take those men back to jail quickly! At once! Clear the courtroom!"

The order simply could not be carried out "at once." For twenty minutes, the militiamen fought with the enraged crowd, and it was not until they confronted the mob with a hedge of glistening bayonets that they managed to drive a wedge through the angry mass and lodge the Renos in jail. The brothers had been held in $63,000 bail each, a prohibitive amount in those days; and on August 4, guarded by militia and heavily armed deputies, they were transported to the supposedly stronger jail at New Albany to await trial.

Frank Reno and the members of the gang who had fled to Canada were still at large. The Pinkertons finally located them in Windsor, just across the narrow Detroit River from Detroit. Windsor was then a Canadian version of Dodge City, a rough and lawless border town, a perfect haven for American desperadoes who had committed every crime from train robbery and forgery to murder.

Pat O'Neil, a young Pinkerton agent who became known to the mobsters as "the Pinkerton Kid," had been investigating a train robbery near Garrison, New York, in which $11,000 had been taken from a safe of the Union Express Company. He tracked his suspects to Windsor and found the town swarming with American thugs. They had literally taken over the Windsor Turf Club, a combination saloon and pool hall, and they had other hangouts in saloons near the Windsor ferry, the connecting link with Detroit.

O'Neil recognized Jack Friday, a Reno henchman, in

Rockford's saloon near the ferry, and Friday, it appears, also spotted him. A fight followed. O'Neil was battered with a pool cue, and Friday finally escaped by leaping through a door, "taking the panels with him." In his report to Allan Pinkerton, O'Neil wrote that the gangsters in the saloon wanted to kill him on the spot, but Tom Manning, the owner of the dive, persuaded them to let him go. Manning told them that if they killed O'Neil, "Pinkerton would never let them rest until he ran all of them down."

The hide-out of Frank Reno and his mob had now been discovered, thanks to "the Pinkerton Kid." Allan Pinkerton, obtaining Canadian warrants for their arrest, led a large posse of his men, including O'Neil, and a number of local deputies, in a raid on a small frame house that the outlaws had made their headquarters. He bagged Frank Reno, Albert Perkins, Charlie Anderson, and the onetime psalm-singing Michael Rogers.

Now the difficulties began. When the prisoners were arraigned, Rogers insisted that he was the victim of mistaken identity. Unfortunately, Pinkerton had no rogues' gallery photograph to link Rogers with his past—and the art of fingerprinting was still unknown. Pinkerton described the manner in which Rogers had been arrested with other members of the gang for the Magnolia robbery, but the judge, thinking the evidence insufficient, "reluctantly" released Rogers for the time being. Pinkerton warned that Rogers would flee the court's jurisdiction, and the ex-churchman promptly made a true prophet of him by skipping over the border back to the states.

Frank Reno, Perkins, and Anderson were still held, and

they became the center of a legal battle that involved chancelleries on both sides of the Atlantic. Extradition warrants had to be obtained from the Canadian government so that the prisoners could be brought back to the United States for trial. This should have been a relatively simple matter, but was not. Pinkerton found himself enmeshed in red tape everywhere he turned. The State Department in Washington, the Governor-General of Canada, and finally even the highest levels of the British government in London became embroiled in the controversy over the extradition of the Reno gunmen.

In the meantime, American blackguards in Windsor planned the assassination of Allan Pinkerton. Dick Barry, a safecracker by profession, was elected to be the triggerman. Barry shadowed Pinkerton on a trip from Windsor to Detroit; and as Pinkerton walked down the ramp of the ferry on the American side, Barry aimed a pistol at the back of his head.

Pinkerton heard the faint click as Barry cocked his weapon, whereupon the veteran detective, still lightning fast in his reactions, whirled and grabbed for the gun. He got his fingers in the trigger guard, wrenched the weapon from Barry's hand, and beat the safecracker into subjection in a short, fierce struggle. Then he handcuffed Barry and marched him through Detroit streets to police headquarters.

Shortly afterward, a train robber named Johnson made a second attempt on Pinkerton's life. He fired a shot at the detective, but missed. He, too, was caught, disarmed, and taken to the police station. Two hours later he escaped. Furious, Pinkerton demanded an explanation and was blandly told by a deputy sheriff that Johnson had fled "while taking a buggy ride around the city." Bribery obviously worked wonders in those days.

The plot got thicker and thicker. Barry, the safecracker whom Pinkerton had subdued, testified at his trial for attempted murder that he had been put up to it by William P. Wood, then head of the U. S. Secret Service. In Washington, Wood indignantly denied the charge, but Barry insisted his trial testimony had been true. One thing was certain: strange things continued to happen.

After almost endless delays, Canadian officials finally agreed to turn the prisoners over to Pinkerton. Allan wired William to send a seagoing tug to Windsor to pick up the party. Reno, Perkins, and Anderson—all handcuffed and leg-shackled—were placed aboard the tug, guarded by a swarm of Pinkertons; and on October 7, a beautiful Indian summer day, the tug left the Windsor dock for what should have been a brief, uneventful trip to Detroit.

But nothing was to be routine about this adventure. The tug was only part way across the Detroit River on this sunny day, with hardly a ripple on the water and visibility perfect, when a steamer bore down upon it and sheared off its bow. The tug went to the bottom like a rock, and the Pinkertons found themselves floundering in the water, trying desperately to hold up the heads of their manacled and helpless prisoners. The steamer, its own bow badly dented, finally rescued them and took them all to Detroit. It strains belief that such a mishap, on such a day, could have been entirely accidental, but William Pinkerton always asserted his conviction that it was —that the collision had resulted from a mixup of seagoing signals.

Allan Pinkerton, suffering from a heavy cold as a result of his dunking in the chill waters, turned his prisoners over to Floyd County Sheriff Thomas J. Fullenlove, who incarcerated them in the New Albany jail along with William and Simeon Reno.

With the Renos all in one place, New Albany became an inviting target in the open warfare between the lawless and the lynch-minded citizens who for so long had been the gang's victims. Average persons, caught in the middle between these two hostile forces, lived in terror.

The Democratic Party, holding a convention in New Albany, actually offered Sheriff Fullenlove a thousand dollars to "let the Seymour Committee get the Renos." The sheriff, an honest and courageous man—though, as events would show, a decidedly overconfident one—spurned the lynch bribe and proclaimed: "There will be no murder for any amount of money . . . the law must take its course . . ."

In the mood of the time, there was little chance of achieving evenhanded justice. Followers of the Reno gang waged a war of terror on the community. Men were waylaid and savagely beaten. Rocks wrapped in paper were hurled through the windows of officials' homes, bearing the message: "If the Renos are lynched you die." Women were threatened. They were warned that they and their children would be kidnaped if their husbands rode with the vigilantes.

On December 7, George Flanders, the honest engineer who had foiled Moore's plot, died of his wound. Murder was now added to the conspiracy and robbery charges against the Renos. This was the only spark needed to ignite the passions of the countryside.

At midnight, December 12, the Jefferson–Indianapolis train—running without headlights, bell, or whistle—crept ghostlike into the sleeping town. Men wearing red flannel masks poured out of it in single file and lined up in a semblance of military order. They carried shotguns, Colt revolvers, and rifles; and they filed briskly, silently, almost like Indians, through the deserted streets. A messenger came up and reported that all the telegraph wires had been cut. New Albany was isolated.

There were only two guards to protect the two-story stone jail. One, Luther (Chuck) Whitten, had been stationed at the curb outside as a lookout; he had started a tiny fire and was warming himself, when he found himself suddenly surrounded by masked men. Breaking free, he ran toward the jail, shouting the alarm; but he was quickly caught and subdued.

His cries had awakened the overconfident Sheriff Fullenlove, who ran from his quarters in the jail, shouting: "I am the Sheriff, the highest peace officer in the county. . . . You must respect the law . . ." He was answered by a volley of shots, and Fullenlove fell, one arm shattered by bullets.

"Don't kill him," the leader of the masked men ordered. "Take him to his house."

The gunning down of the sheriff and the capture of Whitten left only Tom Matthews to protect the jail. Matthews shouted that he would shoot the first man who attempted to enter, but he soon saw that he was helpless before the masked mob that confronted him. He yielded, and the raiders, carrying ropes for their hanging mission, swept into the cellblock.

Frank Reno, a powerful man, put up a fierce struggle, but was buried under the mass of assailants. He was dragged out into the corridor, a noose around his neck. The end of the rope was flung over a beam, and Frank Reno was jerked into space.

Above him, in the second tier of the cellblock, William and Simeon Reno watched in horror. Then the raiders came for them, too. William was dragged from his cell and hanged beside his brother. Simeon struggled so furiously that he had to be knocked unconscious by a blow from the butt of a heavy Colt; then he, too, was hoisted on the beam from which his brothers' bodies already dangled.

Charlie Anderson was the next victim. He begged and pleaded: "My soul, gentlemen, my soul. Give me time to pray for it."

"Ain't worth praying for, Charlie," the vigilante leader told him—and Anderson, too, was lofted into space.

Bloodthirsty now, some of the vigilantes wanted to clean out the cellblock and lynch everyone in the prison. But their stern leader, whom they called "Number One," held them in leash. "We did what we came for," he told them. "Now let's go."

As silently as they had come, the masked vigilantes filed through the deserted streets, boarded their waiting train, and made off into the night. Behind them, in the jail they had raided, one final scene of horror was being enacted.

The rope around Simeon Reno's neck had been a bit too long. His toes just barely touched the floor, and he had not been strangled instantly. As ten other terrified prisoners watched, Simeon regained consciousness from the blow on his head and began to struggle for life. For nearly a half hour, his eyes bulging, his mouth gasping for air, he tried to boost himself on his toes enough to relieve the strangling pressure of the noose about his neck. It was a futile struggle. Slowly, inexorably, the life was squeezed out of him, and he dangled limp beside the bodies of Frank and William.

The lynchings sent a shock wave through the state and nation—and even caused an international uproar. Laura Ellen Reno, the bandits' sister, her eyes red from weeping, went to the jail to claim their bodies. When she saw their purpled, swollen faces, she screamed, rushed to the windows, and shrieked to the mob of curious spectators outside that their blood was on the heads of all.

Allan and William Pinkerton met with the governor, and the appropriate, shocked official statement was issued. It pledged prosecution of the vigilantes; but, as everyone knew, these were empty words—nothing would ever be done. The citizens and officials of the state breathed a collective sigh of relief that the violent Renos had been dispatched, whatever the means.

The international reaction was more serious. Great Britain, through the Canadian Governor-General, demanded an apology for "the shocking and indefensible lynching." There was talk that the British might revoke the extradition treaty, an action that would have made all Canada a safe haven for American miscreants. To forestall this, Congress rushed through a bill pledging federal protection for all extradited criminals in the future; and Secretary of State Seward sent a

copy of this act to London, along with the American apology.

The sensation gradually faded into history. The Renos were
gone, and an uneasy peace, compounded of exhaustion and
relief, descended on the states of the Middle Border.

9

Labor
Strife

ALLAN PINKERTON, that man of
iron, was in the end only human. He had driven himself to
the outermost limits of physical endurance for years, and in
the late summer of 1869 he paid the price. He was dictating
a letter to his secretary when, in midsentence, he had a stroke
that nearly killed him.

His capable sons, William and Robert, attempted for business reasons to minimize the seriousness of his illness. They
pictured their father as only temporarily incapacitated and
still able to oversee the activities of the agency, now nationally
publicized as "The Eye That Never Sleeps."

Yet the truth was that, for more than a year, Allan Pinkerton was so paralyzed that he could not walk or talk. His doc-
tors, the best his fortune could hire, predicted he would be
confined to a wheel chair for the rest of his life, a helpless
hulk. Months of treatment in New York did him no good, and
he returned to Chicago an invalid.

Deep inside this unconquerable man, however, there still lived the iron determination that had marked his entire career. He would *not* remain a helpless cripple; he *would* walk, talk, write again. He began to take daily baths in a crude Michigan spring whose waters were supposed to have curative powers. Day after day, he literally dragged himself into the water; he willed, struggled, forced his immobilized limbs to begin to move again. The muscles began to twitch, began to respond. He reached the point where he could stand again upon his feet, where he could force his reluctant legs to move. Each day he increased the distance he struggled, first to feet, then to yards, then to miles. By September 1870, his handwriting still shaky and spidery, he was informing a friend: "I walk every day eight, ten and twelve miles . . ."

His recovery was little short of miraculous, a tribute to his never-say-die spirit, but it was never to be complete. One side would always remain partially paralyzed; his writing was uncertain; and when he became excited, his speech slurred. But his mind was as keen as ever, and he was able once more to keep his ever-watchful eye on the agency's activities.

He had hardly returned to his desk in 1871 when the great Chicago fire wiped out large portions of the city, including the headquarters of Pinkerton's National Detective Agency. Destroyed in the conflagration were Pinkerton's massive Civil War files and, even more important, his pioneering and invaluable rogues' gallery, containing the pictures and criminal records that had played such important roles in breaking case after case.

Even this final blow could not daunt Pinkerton. Neither stroke nor fire was going to defeat *him*. He began to rebuild the agency's headquarters almost the minute the embers of the fire had cooled, and he wrote the veteran George Bangs: "I will never be beaten, never. Not all the Furies of Hell will stop me from rebuilding *immediately*." He underlined the last word heavily.

To stroke and fire there was now added a third calamity—depression. One of the worst panics in the nation's history broke out in September 1873, when Jay Cooke, the Wall Street finagler, went into bankruptcy. The collapse of Jay Cooke & Co. touched off a chain reaction. Brokerage houses collapsed; there were runs on banks; money went into hiding; and in the last three months of 1873, more than five thousand businesses closed their doors. The blight of depression, the worst that had been experienced up to that time, left the nation prostrate.

Allan Pinkerton, with an eye to drumming up business in a bad time, wrote to George Bangs in the fall of 1873; he suggested that Bangs call upon Franklin Benjamin Gowen, president of the Philadelphia and Reading Railroad, "to suggest something to Mr. Gowen about one thing or another which could be feasible and I have no doubt he would give us work."

The result was to be the Pinkertons' involvement in the prosecution of the Molly Maguires.

Bangs's visit to Gowen came at a time when the railroad tycoon had a pressing need for detective services: murder and terror were rife in the Pennsylvania coal fields. This turmoil was of special concern to Gowen, for he had used his railroad's resources to buy up vast tracts of mining land. He had calculated not only on making a profit from the mines, but on giving his railroad extra revenue from hauling the coal the mines produced.

This scheme, in which one hand would wash the other, had seemed almost foolproof, but the crash of 1873 and the desperately hard times it caused had triggered something akin to insurrection in the coal fields. Gowen and other brutal employers of his stripe began to reap the whirlwind they had sown by some of the most inhuman labor policies the nation has known. Naturally, however, human nature being what it is, Gowen and his fellow executives were not about to recognize their own responsibility for the revolt. They were simply outraged and wanted to put down the rebellion—and so Gowen hired the Pinkertons to track down the ringleaders. The exposure of the Molly Maguires followed.

This was a secret organization that had been formed originally in Ireland to battle large landowners. It had been imported to America along with the great wave of Irish immigration that followed the potato famine of the late 1840s. Thousands of the new Irish immigrants, illiterate and capable only of the crudest manual labor, had gravitated to the coal mining regions. There they were confronted with multiple prejudices—prejudice against foreigners, against themselves as Irish, and against the Catholic religion most of them professed. And there, too, they were ground down and oppressed by callous employers.

They lived in company owned towns. They had to purchase food and supplies from the company store. However much they earned, the company managed to doctor the records so that they were often charged every penny of their wages; they were left with nothing. One miner—and this was typical—who had earned $35.03 was presented with company bills that totaled precisely $35.03.

There were no safety or child labor laws. In 1871, 112 miners were killed and 339 permanently injured in accidents in Pennsylvania coal mines. In seven years, the toll had been: 566 killed, 1,665 permanently injured. One compilation, considered reliable, reported that, of 22,000 coal miners employed in Schuylkill County in 1871, 5,500 were between the ages of seven and sixteen.

Living lives of desperation, workers had no choice but to accept the lot fate had dished out to them. If they protested by striking, mine owners had only to cable Europe for a new horde of immigrants—within a fortnight they would have an army of newcomers whom they could use as strikebreakers to work the mines while the men whose jobs were taken looked on, helpless.

Driven to extremity by injustice, the men turned to violence. It was inevitable; in such circumstances, hate seeks the only available outlet, wreaking vengeance upon property and person in a carnival of destruction and murder. Secret societies, with their mumbo jumbo of oaths and passwords and sworn blood brotherhood, become the ideal vehicles of vendetta. In Pennsylvania, this role was filled by the Molly Maguires.

There was, as can be seen from this background, a mixture of motives, not all of them idealistic. The passions of oppressed laborers intermingled and became confused with emotions aroused by racial and religious hatred—and even personal grudges. As a result, an argument has raged ever since about the true role of the Molly Maguires. Were they plain and simple terrorists? Or were they, as some contend, labor leaders driven to violence by insufferable conditions? The debate has been endless, but one thing at least the record makes clear: the Molly Maguires murdered anyone who, for whatever reason, happened to cause their enmity.

In just sixty days between mid-April and mid-June 1870, the following crimes had been committed in just one coal mining county: the Silver Creek Colliery foreman had been shot from ambush; Gowen himself had been attacked on the highway by armed men; a merchant had been shot on the streets of Tamaqua; a bridge watchman had been beaten by thugs; shots had been fired into the home of a colliery superintendent; the breaker at the Mahanoy City mine had been burned; a mine superintendent had been waylaid and beaten; a farmer had been fatally wounded on the highway; a mine boss had been murdered.

With violence mounting in 1873, Gowen followed up his talk with Bangs by writing Pinkerton to come to Philadelphia for a consultation. Benjamin Franklin, Pinkerton's Philadelphia superintendent, went with his boss to discuss the situation with Gowen. The railroad president described for them the reign of terror in the coal regions and said he wanted to bring the leaders of the Molly Maguires to justice. Uniformed police and other private detectives, he explained, had failed to penetrate the core of the secret society.

Pinkerton agreed to take on the task under certain conditions. He had to be given time. There must be no reference to him, his agency, or any of his men in the company's books. Pinkerton's reports were to be seen only by Gowen. And the agency's undercover men were not to be compelled to take the witness stand. To all of this, Gowen agreed.

The problem now was to find the right agent. Pinkerton was mulling the problem over after his return to Chicago when, while riding to work one morning, he noticed one of his own men who was acting in the role of a trolley car conductor. This agent was James McParland, twenty-nine, thin and red-haired, an immigrant from Ulster who had been on the Pinkerton force for only a year. "Just the man!" Pinkerton decided in a flash of intuition.

He called in McParland and described the hazardous project. Pinkerton told McParland that he was perfectly free to turn down the assignment (no black mark would go against his name in the Pinkerton records); on the other hand, this was a major and important task, one that might be the making of his career if McParland decided to take it. McParland didn't hesitate; he accepted the challenge.

On October 27 a strange, tramplike figure appeared in the Pennsylvania coal regions. He was dressed in an old gray coat, brown pants, a black vest, a gray shirt, a red comforter. He smoked a cutty pipe and had a ten days' growth of beard. He was, he said, James McKenna, a poor boy from Colorado looking for work. In the first of the innumerable saloons he was to frequent during the next months, the German proprietor took one look at him, decided he was in truth a tramp —and threw him out. A fellow Irishman, who had witnessed the scene, took pity on him and conducted him to a railroad boardinghouse.

It was a beginning. The undeniably Irish "James McKenna," trading on the clannishness of his fellow countrymen, gradually widened his circle of acquaintances. He became a familiar figure in the saloons of the coal mining country. He impersonated a happy-go-lucky drunk who possessed a good singing voice and could dance a jig. In his cups, he often set up drinks for all the boys at the bar, and he explained his possession of ready cash by intimating that he had committed some crimes that had culminated in a murder in Buffalo—and so was on the lam from the law.

One thing led to another, and by December 15 McParland had ingratiated himself so well that he obtained a letter of introduction to Muff Lawler, the Body Master (or boss) of the Mollies in Shenandoah, a town twenty miles north of Pottsville. He went there, looking for Lawler, and in a saloon a man named Durkin gave him what McParland recognized as a secret sign of the order.

"Do you know anything about it?" Durkin asked.

"Not just at present, but in the old times I was well posted," McParland told him, intimating that he had belonged to the Mollies in Ireland. Lawler wasn't around, but Durkin told him he should meet Jack Kehoe, who kept the Hibernian House.

They went to Kehoe's. Kehoe was probably the major force in the Mollies at that time. He was forty-three, and he was related by marriage to several families who included among their numbers some of the most ruthless gunmen in the region. Kehoe was both tough and smart.

He gave McParland a sign that the agent failed to recognize.

"I see you know nothing at present," Kehoe remarked, staring at McParland with cold, hard eyes.

McParland realized that he was not dealing with the kind of gullible Irishman he had so easily hoodwinked in the last few weeks, and he felt his throat tighten with a spasm of fear.

"It's a long time since I was within," he told Kehoe as casually as he could.

Kehoe let the matter drop, but McParland had the apprehensive feeling that Kehoe was a man not totally convinced.

It was January 24, 1874, before McParland caught up with Muff Lawler in Shenandoah. Times were hard, the miners were threatening to strike, and there had been a report in the evening paper that Gowen was going to bring in five thousand new immigrants to work the mines. Lawler was incensed.

"It will take the State Militia and all his time and skills to protect his own life," he muttered.

McParland was spending so much money in the saloons that he was afraid of arousing suspicion. And so he kept alluding to those mythical crimes he was supposed to have committed in Buffalo; and, as a further coverup, he intimated that some of his old contacts were using him to dispose of counterfeit bills. This last excuse served a dual purpose. McParland just had to get away at times to keep in contact with Franklin, the Pinkerton superintendent in Philadelphia, and so he could attribute his occasional disappearances from the coal regions to the necessity of meeting his "contact" to obtain more of the "queer."

McParland's free spending and jolly cavorting earned him friends. Lawler was so taken with him that he invited him to his own home. Mrs. Lawler, too, liked him, and McParland ended up boarding with the Lawlers.

Franklin wanted daily reports, a requirement that put an added strain on McParland, who shared a room with a Molly and had almost no privacy. The situation was eased somewhat when Lawler discovered McParland could write and had him act as secretary in preparing the Body Master's correspondence. This role gave McParland access to writing materials without arousing suspicion.

Mailing the letters to Franklin was more difficult. McParland would wander at night into nearby towns and drop his reports secretly into a mailbox, or sometimes, if he was lucky enough to spot a mail truck making its pickups, he would simply toss the letter on the floor of the truck and walk on.

In February, Lawler finally got him a job in the mines. McParland handled twenty tons of coal in each ten-hour shift. The job did not last long. On February 17, McParland's hands were badly crushed in an accident, and he could no longer work. During his brief stint in the colliery, however, he had met a man who was to become important to him, Frank Macandrew. From him, McParland learned that Lawler had proposed him for membership in the Mollies.

The Mollies' Council met at Lawler's on the night of April 14. Macandrew waited downstairs with McParland for the decision. It was an anxious, nail-biting time. Would "James McKenna" be made a member of the Mollies? Or would he be exposed as a spy—and condemned to death? One of the Mollies in the meeting finally came downstairs with the word: McParland had been accepted. That night, he reported triumphantly to Franklin: "So you see the victory is won at last."

Not quite. McParland had his foot in the door that would

lead to victory, but there were to be many anxious, cliff-hanging moments, with his life in the balance, before the final triumph.

The excessive nightly drinking, combined with the strain of playing spy, finally undermined even McParland's stout constitution. He became ill, too ill even to think of working again soon; and so, when he had partially recovered, Lawler sent him to contact other Body Masters in Wilkes-Barre, Kingston, Plymouth, and Scranton. In Scranton, McParland attended a meeting of twenty-five Body Masters, and shortly afterward he disappeared, ostensibly to get some more of the "queer." Actually, he skipped into Philadelphia and gave Franklin a list of names of all the Mollies he had identified, their ranks in the organization, and their remuneration.

So far, McParland had uncovered no evidence of violence, but that was now to come. A Welshman, Gomer James, had shot and killed a Molly. This seems to have been the result of a personal grudge and had nothing to do with the cause of labor. The Mollies were nevertheless determined to avenge their fallen comrade. Lawler was ordered to have two gunmen kill James the minute he was released on bail; but Lawler had little stomach for murder and kept putting off the deed.

Lawler's procrastination made him unpopular, and Barney Dolan, the ranking Molly in the county, came to Shenandoah on July 15 to oust Lawler as Body Master. Whom did he propose to install in Lawler's place? None other than the popular "James McKenna"!

McParland almost fainted from the shock. It took three days of heavy drinking and fast talking for him to worm his way out of the appointment. He kept pointing out that he was "wanted" for that old "murder" in Buffalo, and he argued it just wouldn't do, either for him or the Mollies, if he were made Body Master. This logic finally prevailed, and Macandrew was named to succeed Lawler. But since Macandrew was illiterate, McParland was appointed secretary.

Secretly, McParland notified Franklin of the plot against Gomer James, suggesting that James be arrested or urged to leave the neighborhood to save his life. Macandrew, like Lawler, hesitated about carrying out the order for James's execution, but the pressure within the Mollies mounted. In August, Barney Dolan was expelled, and the steely-eyed Kehoe succeeded him as the top Molly in the county. Almost at once, McParland became aware that Kehoe was eying him as the prospective assassin of James. McParland escaped the assignment only by getting himself so roaring drunk that it was obvious he was not to be trusted to pull off "a clean job."

Violence now mounted in the coal regions. By November 1874, Gowen and the other mine owners were putting the squeeze on the workers. The owners had formed a solid bloc. When the miners asked for more money, the owners offered only pay cuts, accompanied by the threat that any miner who didn't accept the proposed slash would be blackballed and find himself out of work entirely.

Hardly a day passed now without some explosion of savagery. In just three days in mid-November, this was the toll: a Molly was found dead in the streets of Carbondale, north of Scranton; a man had his throat cut; another was crucified in the woods; a mining boss was beaten up; a man was murdered in Scranton; and another Molly, named Dougherty, was the target of an attempted assassination by one W. M. (Bully Bill) Thomas.

Driven to desperation, the miners went on strike. By the first of January 1875, nearly all of the mines had been closed; the so-called "Long Strike" had begun. McParland circulated widely through the seething colliery area, and some of his reports must have been unpleasant reading for Gowen. In one, he bluntly told the railroad president that "all classes" of persons "are very much embittered toward your company and openly denounce the course you have taken." He warned that attacks on mining properties would almost certainly follow.

Gowen responded by sending waves of newly recruited strikebreakers into the mines. And the strikers, Mollies among them, reacted as McParland had predicted. On the last day of March, the Summit telegraph office was burned and a train derailed. Angry Mollies wanted to destroy the railroad bridge across the Susquehanna River, and McParland, using every pretext he could think of, had the devil's own time talking them out of it.

The final crisis was approaching, and McParland slipped into Philadelphia for a conference with Franklin and Allan Pinkerton, who had come down from Chicago. After listening to McParland, Pinkerton advised Franklin to add six Pinkertons to the Coal and Iron Police at Pottsville. The Pinkertons would be there to protect mine properties—and, in effect, the strikebreakers brought in to work them. Robert J. Linden, Pinkerton's assistant superintendent in Chicago, was called to head the new Pinkerton mine squad, and he was informed of

McParland's activities and told to keep in close touch with the man known to the Mollies as James McKenna.

The State Militia were now called out to join the Coal and Iron Police and the Pinkertons. The miners were beaten. They offered to end their strike for a contract providing a flat weekly wage of fifteen dollars for six eight-hour days; but the owners rejected even that and sent more strikebreakers into the mines. The Mollies rallied in the hills, joined by miners of every ethnic origin, and on the morning of June 3 they attempted to storm the West Shenandoah Colliery at Reading. Leading the angry mob, with a worn gray coat flapping about his knees, brandishing a hickory club and with two pistols stuck in his belt, was "James McKenna." Linden and eighteen of his Iron and Coal Police confronted the rioters with deadly, leveled rifles; and the mob, its nerve broken, retreated. "James McKenna" brought up the rear, shouting curses over his shoulder.

Unable to wreak vengeance on the heavily armed mine owners, the Mollies turned to the settling of private grudges. Their first target was Bully Bill Thomas. Macandrew told McParland that Thomas Hurley and two other men had been assigned to take out Thomas. McParland tried desperately to get off a warning message to Franklin, but he had no opportunity. Perhaps some Mollies were already having doubts about him. At any rate, an obviously suspicious Molly stuck to him shadow-close throughout the night, and McParland was helpless. The following morning, a messenger arrived from Hurley saying that Bully Bill Thomas had been killed.

The report was not quite accurate. Hurley and his two gunmen had surprised Thomas at the door of a stable, shot him down, and left him for dead. They were not aware until two days later that Thomas, though badly wounded, had survived.

This bungled attempt seems only to have revived the long-standing agitation for the killing of Gomer James, who had left the area for a time after McParland's first warning but had now returned. Macandrew scheduled the event for a Fourth of July picnic taking place on Monday night, July 5. On that same date, Gowen was invading the hostile mining country to speak at Pottsville, and there were fears that an attempt would be made on his life. McParland, trying to keep track of the multiple threats, had just too much on his hands. Murder got away from him.

Some of the Mollies hated Benjamin Yost, a town night watchman in Tamaqua who had given them trouble. About 2 A.M. July 6, as Yost was climbing a ladder propped against a lamppost to adjust a street lamp, he was shot and mortally wounded. His wife, watching from a front window of their home, saw two men running from the scene.

McParland went into Tamaqua on July 15 and began to circulate among his Molly acquaintances. Some months earlier, at a wedding, he had met Mary Ann Higgins, a pretty, lively, blue-eyed girl who was James Kerrigan's sister-in-law. Kerrigan shared Body Master status in Tamaqua with James Carroll, and Mary Ann lived with the Kerrigans. "James McKenna" now began to "spark" Mary Ann, and Kerrigan found the pair holding hands on his porch almost every night.

With this romance helping to allay suspicion, McParland soon got Kerrigan to talk. The Body Master boasted about his role in the Yost murder and even showed McParland his .32 caliber revolver, which, he said, was one of the weapons that had done the job. Alec Campbell, another ranking Molly, also confided to McParland that he had helped mastermind the slaying, and he introduced the detective to Hugh McGehan and James Boyle as the pair who had actually shot Yost. On another occasion, James Carroll showed McParland a revolver belonging to James Roarity which he said had also been used in the slaying; and, somewhat later, Alec Campbell announced that he was so pleased with McGehan for his sterling work in the Yost case that he was rewarding the slayer by setting him up with a saloon of his own.

While McParland was engaged in tracking down this evidence and trying to get corroboration for the various stories, Gomer James, so long threatened, finally got a lethal dose of lead. He was tending bar at a fire department picnic on August 16 when he was gunned down in plain view of scores of witnesses, none of whom dared talk. "James McKenna" promptly dropped the hand of the enchanting Mary Ann Higgins and hurried back to Shenandoah, where he soon wangled a confidence out of Thomas Hurley. Hurley bragged that he was the man who had killed James.

McParland's role was becoming ever more difficult. He had been seen talking to Linden; and, though he had pretended to quarrel furiously with the Pinkerton detective, suspicions had been aroused. Now, when murder was afoot, trusted Mollies stuck to McParland day and night, never letting him out of their sight; and, as McParland discovered too late, he was also being cut out of the chain of information about premurder planning sessions. As a result, the murder of two mine bosses, Tom Sanger and J. P. Jones, caught him by surprise.

The Jones killing was especially brazen. The mine boss had spent the night of September 1 at his home in Lansford and had gone to the railroad depot at seven o'clock the following morning to catch the train to Tamaqua. There, in full view of some hundred persons, all friendly to him, he was gunned down on the platform by a three-man murder squad headed by James Kerrigan.

The killers walked unhurriedly away and might have escaped entirely except for a foolish mistake. They decided to go to Kerrigan's home in Tamaqua to get some liquor to celebrate. Unfortunately for them, the Tamaqua train Jones was to have taken brought word of his killing to the crowd on the station platform. As in the case of the Renos, the unchecked carnival of murder began to build its own lynch-minded counterforce. Kerrigan, the known Body Master, was immediately suspected; a posse was formed; and Kerrigan and his two gunmen, Michael Boyle and Edward Kelly, were seized in a cemetery where they had been drinking toasts to the morning's deed.

Angry mobs at Tamaqua and Lansford threatened to lynch them out of hand, but the three men were put aboard a special train and carried safely to jail in Mauch Chunk. Campbell immediately went to work to establish alibis for the arrested men, but the Mollies were soon stunned by the word that Kerrigan had admitted all and agreed to become a witness for the state.

The vigilante flame, once fanned, was not to be easily extinguished. On December 10, a mob stormed a house in Wiggin's Patch near Mahanoy City, a few miles east of Shenandoah. The building was occupied by the O'Donnell and McAllister families, both related by marriage to Jack Kehoe. The masked raiders, firing indiscriminately, killed Charles O'Donnell and Mrs. Charles McAllister. Friday O'Donnell and Charles McAllister were wounded, but managed to escape.

When McParland learned of the raid, he was furious. He wrote an angry letter to Franklin, declaring he was quitting the case because he wanted no part in the shooting of women. "If I was not here the Vigilante Committee would not know who was guilty and when I find them shooting women in their thirst for blood I hereby tender my resignation to take effect as soon as this message is received," he wrote. It took all of Franklin's persuasive powers to induce him to stay with the case a little longer.

In any event, time was running out for McParland. Kehoe had become convinced that a spy had wormed his way into the ranks of the Mollies, and his hard, suspicious eyes fastened on "James McKenna." When Molly after Molly was arrested, based on the secret information McParland had furnished, suspicion became almost a certainty. Kehoe told Macandrew that "James McKenna" was a detective, and Macandrew quoted Kehoe as saying: "Macandrew, for God's sake, have him killed this night, or he will hang half the people in Schuylkill County."

Instead, Macandrew warned McParland, and the detective decided his only chance was to try to brazen things out. He confronted Kehoe and demanded that he be brought to trial before the Mollies so that he could prove his innocence. Kehoe, cold and hard, promised a hearing, but later called it off. It became obvious that the only "hearing" for McParland would be from guns in the hands of Molly killers. The detective, living in fear that any minute might be his last, changed his regular itinerary, but found that he was being followed almost everywhere he went. He had to get away, and on March 7, 1876, almost three years after he had begun his hazardous assignment, he left the coal regions for good and returned to Philadelphia.

Gowen, who had been a district attorney before he went into railroading and coal mining, had been named a special prosecutor to try the arrested Mollies. He and Allan Pinkerton knew that McParland's direct testimony from the stand was essential. Would McParland take the risk and give it? The detective considered for five minutes, then said he would.

The sudden appearance of "James McKenna" at the trial of the murderers of Yost struck the Mollies dumb. They might have suspected, but they had not *known*. The Pottsville *Times* of May 8 described the courtroom scene this way: "Carroll was as if struck by lightning. Boyle shook like an aspen, as the prosecutor announced, 'We will produce to you the full and complete confession of James Carroll and Hugh McGehan of their part of this murder as made to James McKenna, a detective,' whom they knew by that name but whose real name was James McParland."

McParland proved as formidable on the witness stand as he had been daring and resourceful in his undercover assignment. Through a whole series of trials, under relentless hammering by defense attorneys, he remained unshaken; not once was he tripped up. And the result was that nineteen Mollies were convicted and went to the gallows.

The Pinkertons' role in the case has been frequently denounced—and just as strongly defended. But there can be no doubt that the Pinkertons had enlisted on the side of repressive employers. Between 1866 and 1892, they were hired to protect property in some seventy other strikes. The most notorious incident occurred July 5–6, 1892, at the Carnegie Steel Company plant in Homestead, Pennsylvania. Pinkertons, being brought in by river barge to protect the plant, were attacked by strikers as they attempted to land; and in the pitched battle that followed, four Pinkertons were killed, one hundred wounded, while eight strikers were killed or mortally wounded. The bloody clash touched off a storm of criticism across the nation, aimed at the Pinkertons and the Carnegie executives who had refused to bargain with their workers.

Unquestionably, Allan Pinkerton, the once youthful rebel, was wedded to the propertied classes that were his employers. Yet the story was not entirely one-sided. It was a brutal time in which the workingman was considered to have no rights. Pinkerton joined the conventional wisdom of his day and defended threatened plants and property. He appears not greatly to have concerned himself about the reservations expressed by James McParland in his investigation of the Mollies. McParland was often disgusted with Gowen's tactics and warned that the railroad president's all-out effort to crush the miners with strikebreakers, police, and the state militia would lead inevitably to outrage and violence. The warnings went unheeded—and the violence McParland had foreseen erupted on a shocking scale.

When all of this has been said, however, one clear fact remains: the Molly Maguires were a violent and desperate lot. Many of the murders McParland investigated had no nobler motivation than personal spite; they were not connected with the cause of labor. And there can be no question that the men against whom McParland testified—and whom he sent to the gallows—were guilty of the bloody crimes with which they were charged.

10
The Pinkertons and the Mafia

POLICE CHIEF David Hennessy of New Orleans was a tall, powerfully built man. He had a bristling mustache and cold gray eyes, both indicative of a character that was bold and determined. In law enforcement circles, he was respected for his rock-ribbed integrity and his dauntless courage. Indeed, only such a man could have followed the course that Chief Hennessy took in New Orleans in 1890.

The great Louisiana port city, the key artery in a growing fruit trade with Latin American countries, had fallen under the dominance of the Mafia. This secret criminal society, which rules much of the American underworld today and possesses enormous power, was then relatively unknown to Americans. The Mafia had flourished for centuries in Sicily and had become a criminal government more powerful at times than the established government of the state. In the great wave of Italian immigration to America in the 1870s and 1880s, many Sicilian newcomers, criminals in their homeland, brought with them the Mafia code of *omerta* (the sealing of one's lips before the law no matter what the provocation) and its grim methods of extortion, terror, and murder.

Typical of the new breed of Mafiosi was a famous Sicilian outlaw named Giuseppe Esposito. He had become the center of an international storm by kidnaping and holding an English clergyman for ransom. When the ransom money was not supplied rapidly enough to suit Esposito, he cut off the Englishman's ears and sent them to London as a warning. This was a bit too much. The Italian government, which had not greatly concerned itself about the Mafia, ordered troops into Sicily, and Esposito fled to the United States, where he was smuggled ashore in New Orleans.

There he soon established an American branch of the Mafia. He operated a small logger in the oyster trade, and from its masthead he flew a pennant bearing the letters "Leoni," the name of the Mafia boss of Sicily. Despite this brazenness, Esposito was protected by his band of cutthroats and terrorists, and he soon established a stranglehold over the piers and the hiring of longshoremen.

Chief Hennessy, who owned a private detective agency before he was appointed police chief in 1881, first clashed with the Mafia over Esposito. He vowed to deport the gangster to his native Sicily—and he did. The swarthy, knife-scarred Esposito was arrested, and Hennessy personally escorted him to New York, where he was put aboard a steamship sailing for Italy. There he was convicted as an extortionist and jailed for life.

The downfall of Esposito, colorful episode though it was,

had little effect on the Mafia organization in New Orleans. In the Mafia, the old saying, "The King is dead, long live the King," is a hard fact of life. There is always a new Mafioso eager to fill the shoes of the departed. In New Orleans, the dread society's power became concentrated in the hands of the shipping magnates Antonio and Carlo Matranga, both originally from Palermo. They ruled the port with an iron hand. No banana freighter could unload at the docks without paying them tribute. No longshoreman could get work without the approval of their hiring bosses.

The Matrangas' lucrative rackets rapidly made them millionaires, but it is an axiom of life that when this kind of loot is up for grabs, existence becomes far from peaceful. In the Matrangas' case, their rivals were three brothers—George, Joe, and Peter Provenzano. The Matrangas had driven the Provenzanos off the docks in their thrust for power, and the Provenzanos had gone into the grocery business. But the Mafia, under the leadership of the Matrangas, destroyed their stocks and intimidated their customers. The Provenzanos armed their followers, and warfare followed.

On May 6, 1890, a street gun battle took place between the two Mafia factions. Gangsters on both sides were killed, and innocent pedestrians were hit by wild-flying bullets. Public indignation began to rise, and it was fed by a seemingly endless stream of murders. Hardly a day passed without some gory crime. One Italian, his throat cut, was found floating in a canal. Another, his head almost severed from his body, was found stuffed into a roaring fire in his own fireplace. In all, according to a later tally, there were some ninety-five homicides in New Orleans in 1890, almost all the result of Mafia warfare.

Chief Hennessy vowed to put an end to it. He declared publicly that he would break up the Mafia, and he sent to Italy for the police records of some hundred Mafiosi who were believed to have been smuggled into New Orleans. The chief's campaign against the Mafia was no easy task. Terror sealed the lips of witnesses; even many of the Italian detectives on Hennessy's own force pretended to know nothing, see nothing, hear nothing. Despite such obstacles, Hennessy doggedly built up his case, aided by a few honest subordinates. He was threatened—and he ignored the threats. He was offered bribes—and he scorned the bribes.

Finally, in mid-October 1890, he had his case ready for court. On the night of October 15, he left his office and started to walk home, apparently deep in thought about the testimony he was to give in just two days. It was a dreary night, with a drizzly rain falling. As Chief Hennessy reached the corner of Girod and Basin streets, not far from his home, a thin, piping, boyish whistle sounded along the streets. Almost instantly, shadowy figures sprang out of the night, one wearing a strip of oilcloth as a raincoat. Hennessy was surrounded. There was a blast of shotgun fire, followed by several revolver shots. Then the shadows faded into the night as swiftly as they had appeared.

Hennessy, mortally wounded, staggered a few feet and collapsed across steps leading to a nearby porch. To a neighbor who was the first to reach him, he murmured, "The Dagos did it"—and collapsed. He died about nine o'clock the next morning.

William Pinkerton, in Chicago, was outraged when he read newspaper accounts of the murder. He and Hennessy had been close friends. They were much alike in physique and character, both tall and powerfully built, both dedicated to honest law enforcement. Pinkerton, as he wrote, regarded Hennessy with the kind of affection he might have given a "younger brother," and he was determined to avenge his fallen friend if he could.

William and Robert Pinkerton now headed the agency. Allan Pinkerton, who had struggled on for years after his near-fatal stroke, had finally collapsed in late June 1884 and had died on July 1. His two capable sons inherited an organization unique in the annals of private detective agencies.

The Pinkerton agency, with its massive files on criminals—in the head office in Chicago and the principal branch office in New York—filled a tremendous void in law enforcement. Weak and baffled local police departments turned to it almost automatically for aid in solving difficult and sensational cases. So it was in New Orleans.

The murder of Chief Hennessy had aroused the city. Police, spurred on by an indignant administration and citizenry, rounded up nineteen Mafia suspects, including Joe Macia, head of the Macia Steamship Line, and Carlo Matranga, known as "Millionaire Charlie." It soon became apparent, however, that arrests were one thing, trial and conviction another. Mafia terror began to have its usual effect. Some witnesses faltered and changed their stories; others simply disappeared. The Mafia bragged openly that the arrested men would never be brought to trial.

Officials saw their case crumbling bit by bit every day; and it was just at this time of crisis and despair that William Pinkerton wrote to Colonel William Schaumberg, an old friend who was then secretary to Mayor Joseph Shakespear. "I will do anything in my power," Pinkerton declared, "to bring this murderer to justice, placing my whole Agency at your call."

It was as if FBI Director J. Edgar Hoover, in another and later time, had offered his help to a beleaguered police department. New Orleans welcomed Pinkerton's assistance. And life was never to be quite the same for one of the most remarkable detectives the Pinkertons ever produced.

Francis P. Dimaio was in his late twenties at the time. He was slenderly but strongly built, with olive skin, dark brown eyes and a crown of thick black hair that was to earn him his Mafia nickname, "the Raven." Dimaio had joined the Pinkerton agency in 1886. In the fall of 1890 he'd been married for just six months, but was so busy working on an insurance fraud case out of the Philadelphia office that he and his bride had not had a honeymoon.

They were planning now for their long-delayed lovers' trip and were packing their bags to leave on Saturday, October 22, 1890, when a messenger delivered a note to their door. It was from Superintendent Robert J. Linden, in charge of the Philadelphia office, and it read: "Report to the home of Principal Robert Pinkerton, 81 Eighth Avenue, Brooklyn, tomorrow, Sunday, promptly at 2 P.M."

Once more duty took precedence over romance. Dimaio reluctantly kissed his bride good-by, and the next day, at the appointed hour, he climbed the steps of the Brooklyn brownstone house in which Robert Pinkerton lived. Long years after, in the 1940s, the elderly but still spry Dimaio recalled for author James D. Horan every detail of what happened when the door of Robert Pinkerton's house opened to him.

Standing in the doorway was Henry W. Minster, assistant superintendent of the Philadelphia office. Minster ushered Dimaio into the front parlor. The sun was shining through windows framed by heavy velvet drapes. An oil painting of Allan Pinkerton stared down at the young detective from its place of honor on the wall.

Surprise followed surprise. William Pinkerton, whom Dimaio had never met, entered the room, and Dimaio sensed instantly that a project of unusual importance was in the making. Pinkerton's orders were mysterious and unusual, too. Dimaio was instructed to go to the Bowery and buy a complete set of clothes, including a derby with a New York label. The next day, after spending the night in Robert Pinkerton's home, he was to take a train to Chicago and register at the Brevoort Hotel. William Pinkerton and Minster were going to Washington to confer with the heads of the U. S. Secret Service, and they would later join Dimaio at the Brevoort. Only then would the detective learn the details of his mysterious assignment.

William Pinkerton asked Dimaio, almost as an afterthought, if he was married. "Yes, sir, just six months," Dimaio told him. Pinkerton thought for a moment and then said that the task he had in mind would be extremely dangerous; after Dimaio heard the details in Chicago, he could decline it if he wished and his refusal would not be held against him. But Dimaio, bubbling with the confidence of youth, assured Pinkerton he would accept the assignment, no matter what it was.

When they all met again in Chicago, William Pinkerton unfolded the scheme he had in mind. The New Orleans authorities, he explained, lacked sufficient evidence to convict the killers of Chief Hennessy. There was only one way to get such evidence: an informer would have to be planted in the prison where the Mafia leaders were being held, and he would have to be clever enough to gain their confidence and get the story from their own lips. This was to be Dimaio's assignment.

The young detective, as the Pinkertons had deduced from studying the files of all their operatives, was ideal for this hazardous mission. He was a born actor. In previous cases, he had impersonated a Portuguese seaman, a Latin dance instructor, an Italian immigrant, and an organ-grinder. Now he was to become Anthony Ruggiero, a famous international counterfeiter with a reputation for toughness among the mobs of New York and New Orleans.

Pinkerton had a large file on Ruggiero. It included a rogues' gallery picture and a thorough explanation of his *modus operandi*. Pinkerton, with his usual thoroughness, had checked with Italian police, who reported that Ruggiero had recently been arrested in northern Italy and would be out of circulation for many months. Thus, Dimaio would not risk face-to-face exposure.

For the next few days, Dimaio spent long hours practicing the role he was to play. Minster was both coach and critic. Dimaio would transform himself into Ruggiero and act the way he thought the tough counterfeiter would act in certain circumstances. Minster would find fault, and they would run through the scene again and again. Finally, both became convinced that the impersonation was as realistic as possible. "I stressed habits, special Italian swearwords, the walk and manner of this man I had never met, until they were part of me," Dimaio recalled for Jim Horan years later.

Once Dimaio was proficient in his role, the rest of the plan was put into operation. Pinkerton supplied a suitcase crammed with six thousand dollars in excellent counterfeit bills. Dimaio, acting as Ruggiero would have in similar circumstances, ripped open the lining of his coat and sewed a stack of the bogus money into it. Then, following instructions, he departed for the town of Amite, Louisiana, where he registered at a boardinghouse run by a Mrs. Rogers.

It was here that he was to be arrested by Captain A. F. Wilde, of the Secret Service in New Orleans. William Pinkerton had showed him a picture of Wilde, a tough-looking man with a walrus mustache. Minster accompanied Dimaio as far as Hammond, Louisiana, a town about ten miles from Amite. There he waited for the arrest to take place. As soon as he learned that Wilde had caught "Ruggiero," he was to contact a French attorney in New Orleans. Minster would then return to Chicago, and Dimaio from his prison cell would send him coded letters through the attorney who had been hired to represent him.

The plot worked with clocklike precision. Dimaio had been staying at Mrs. Rogers' boardinghouse for just two days when, as he was about to enter the dining room, he saw "a rural looking gentleman" studying the guest register in which was recorded the name "Anthony Ruggiero of Nashville." Dimaio whirled around and headed for the front door, announcing he was going out to buy some cigars before eating. Wilde moved swiftly, grabbed him, spun him about, and held him at gunpoint. Then the Secret Service agent reached inside Dimaio's jacket, ripped the lining—and out tumbled the hoard of counterfeit bills.

"This man is one of the most notorious counterfeiters in the country," Wilde announced in tones loud enough to be heard by every guest.

Dimaio's valise was brought down from his room. It was opened and more counterfeit bills spilled out, along with a loaded revolver. Mrs. Rogers fainted. The boardinghouse was in an uproar over the arrest of the desperado it had been harboring.

When Wilde took his handcuffed prisoner to the railroad depot to catch a train for New Orleans, a large crowd gathered. Nothing so exciting as this had ever happened in Amite. One spectator became so carried away by the drama that he made a lunge at Dimaio, shouting that he recognized the prisoner as the man who had palmed off a phony twenty dollar bill on him at the St. Louis fair. Dimaio decided it was time to act like the tough Ruggiero. He swung both manacled fists at his accuser and knocked him unconscious. Infuriated, the crowd of onlookers surged forward, ready to lynch Dimaio on the spot; Wilde had all he could do to fight his way through the mob and pitch his prisoner into the caboose that was to take them to New Orleans.

In such fashion, with the name "Ruggiero" in headlines and the account of the desperado's vicious nature growing with each retelling, Dimaio was booked and thrown unceremoniously into the Old Parish Prison, where the Mafia leaders were being held. That night, as Dimaio lay tense and sleepless in the bunk that had been assigned to him, he heard the door of the cellblock open. One of the Italian prisoners whispered, "Who is it?"

Low-voiced came the reply: "It's me, Joe. A government man brought in a counterfeiter; watch out, he may be an informer."

Listening, Dimaio shivered. He realized that even prison employees, some of them, must be on the payroll of the mob.

The next morning, Dimaio learned that "Joe" was a slender, good-looking young Italian named Emanuel Politz—or, as his name was sometimes spelled, Polizzi. He was one of the nineteen who had been charged with Hennessy's murder.

Conditions in the prison, Dimaio quickly discovered, were almost indescribably miserable and filthy. Each man was given a small wooden toilet, nicknamed in macabre fashion the "ice cream freezer." The food was rotten enough to turn the strongest stomach. A man had all he could do just to survive in such circumstances, but Dimaio, in addition, had to worry about the Mafia leaders who sat in a circle at the rear of the cellblock, regarding him suspiciously.

Dimaio had just finished his nauseating breakfast when a prison guard opened the cellblock door and threw in a newspaper.

"There you are, Ruggiero! Read all about yourself," he shouted.

Dimaio had already decided on the tough "Ruggiero" role he would play. As the newspaper fell on his lap, he slapped it angrily away, kicked it across the floor, and cursed colorfully in Italian. Politz picked up the paper, and all the Mafiosi read the account of the counterfeiting desperado who had been plunged into their midst.

That afternoon, Frank Romero, one of the defendants in the Hennessy case, approached Dimaio and tried to begin a conversation. Still acting out the part of tough Tony Ruggiero, Dimaio swung from the floor. His haymaker caught Romero squarely on the jaw and knocked him unconscious across the cellblock.

"Keep away from me," Dimaio snarled, acting like a trapped animal. "The next time—" He left the sentence unfinished, but drew a finger across his throat.

The Italians revived the unconscious Romero by dousing him with water. The gangster, who prided himself upon his toughness, began to shout at once about the terrible things he was going to do to the squirt who had slugged him. Dimaio, in his brash and reckless Ruggiero role, called his bluff. Stalking down the cellblock, he paused and glared down at the angry Romero. "You talking about me?" he demanded. He put such menace into the question that Romero wilted, and one of the other Italians grabbed Dimaio's arm and said, placatingly, "We only want to be friends." Dimaio shook off the friendly hand as if it were a noisome slug and strode back to his own cell.

Fortunately, his cellmate, Billy Weems, a veteran burglar, had witnessed the scene and was greatly impressed. To add to his own stature, he began to make up fanciful tales, which he related to the listening Mafiosi, about how tough Ruggiero was and what a vicious reputation he had in the underworld of New York.

Now began a long siege, an almost superhuman test of endurance. Weeks dragged past while Dimaio continued to live his role of the snarling tough who refused to be friends with anyone. During this period, the rotten prison food threatened to end the detective's life before he could get the confessions he sought. He suffered severe attacks of dysentery and walked about his cell bent over with cramps. He lost so much weight that he seemed little more than a walking skeleton.

He might have died except for a New Orleans madam who had the run of the prison. She had heard about the great New York counterfeiter and expressed a desire to see him. But she was shocked at Dimaio's wasted appearance.

"My God, kid, you look as if you could stand a good feed," she exclaimed. And the next day she sent Dimaio a fried chicken and a bottle of wine.

From that time on, twice each week, the madam sent Dimaio meals prepared in her kitchen. Her kindness probably saved the detective's life because, as Dimaio later said, "I was so weak I couldn't knock over a kitten."

For a month, despite his increasingly desperate physical condition, Dimaio never wavered in his tough-guy impersonation, making it plain he wanted nothing to do with the accused Mafia leaders. His psychology was sound. The more he scorned them, the more convinced they became that he must be a true-blue criminal—and the more anxious they became to make friends. Finally, reluctantly, with a trace of almost royal condescension, Dimaio allowed himself to be persuaded bit by bit. He confided to Romero that he was sorry he had slugged him and allowed Romero and the others to persuade him to accept a bit of the wine and food smuggled into the prison by bribed deputies.

Eager to impress this new friend, the Mafiosi bragged about how tough they were and how they ran the city of New

Orleans. But they steered clear of the subject in which Dimaio was most interested—the Hennessy murder.

The French attorney who had been assigned to represent Dimaio—shocked at his client's appearance—notified Minster in Chicago. Minster in turn advised William Pinkerton that they should pull Dimaio off the case to save his life, but the detective refused to leave the horrible Old Parish Prison. He was picking up scraps of information, and he was convinced that eventually he could break the case.

He wrote down the details that he gathered on small scraps of paper rolled into tiny pellets. These he gave to the French attorney, who forwarded them to Minster. Passing messages right under the eyes of the watching Mafiosi was a hazardous procedure, but there was no help for it. Dimaio knew that if he were furtive, the Mafiosi would become instantly suspicious. It was best to do the thing boldly, without any attempt at concealment; and so he let it be known that he was writing to "a blonde on Basin Street" of whom he was enamored. "Ruggiero's" letters to his "blonde" became a prison joke; and each day, when he retired to a corner of his cell to pen his supposed love letters, bawdy remarks flew about the cellblock about Ruggiero's "blonde" and all the things she must be doing in his absence.

In the notes that Dimaio smuggled out was some information he had gathered about a private detective and a crooked New Orleans attorney, both of whom were bribing state witnesses to leave the city before the Hennessy trial began.

Although Dimaio's situation had been desperate almost from the moment he entered the prison, it now became worse on several counts. His own New Orleans attorney, frightened at the go-between role he was playing, told Dimaio he would no longer represent him. In explanation he drew a finger across his throat, indicating graphically what would happen to him if the Mafia became aware of the role he had played. William Pinkerton came to New Orleans in this crisis and hired another attorney, who was shocked almost speechless when he first met Dimaio.

The dysentery epidemic in the prison had worsened. In addition, Dimaio had contracted malaria. He had wasted away from 185 pounds to 140 and was sometimes too weak to leave his cot. The stench in the prison became unbearable; one day when the kindly madam tried to visit the man she had helped to keep alive, she was forced to cover her nose and face with a handkerchief and flee from this chamber of horrors. The new attorney was equally affected. He reported to Pinkerton that visits to the prison made him physically ill. Again, William Pinkerton wanted to call off the effort and get Dimaio out; but the gallant and stubborn detective refused, insisting that he would stay the course no matter what happened.

He knew, however, that he could not last much longer. He would have to make a move.

During the long weeks of suffering in which he had established his credibility as a genuine tough and allayed suspicion, Dimaio had carefully cultivated the society of young Joe Politz. He sensed that Politz might be the weakest link in the chain of conspiracy, and so he shared his wine with Politz and condescended to accept in return some of the spaghetti that Politz had brought into the prison. Subtly now, he began to work on Politz's nerves.

To lay the groundwork, Dimaio staged a furious argument

with Romero. Politz, curious, naturally wanted to know what had caused the row. Dimaio, the accomplished actor, put on a great show of secrecy. This, naturally, only made Politz more curious and more persistent. Finally, pretending great reluctance, Dimaio let it appear that Politz had persuaded him to change his mind. He swore Politz to secrecy, and then he confided that "the others" were beginning to be afraid that Politz might inform on them. Dimaio said he had defended Politz in his argument with Romero, insisting that Politz could be trusted and would never "go to the law."

Politz was shocked at first—and unbelieving. But Dimaio kept working on him, and Politz gradually became nervous and mistrustful. This showed in his conduct, and the other Italians began to become truly suspicious of him. The tensions in the cellblock, so carefully fostered by Dimaio, were building to the breaking point. All that was needed was one final prick at Politz's jittery nerve endings.

Dimaio's opportunity came late one Sunday afternoon. Politz, as was his custom, had had spaghetti dinners delivered to the prison for himself and Dimaio. The detective was stretched out on his cot, so ill and weak he could hardly move, and so Politz brought the dinners to his cell, sat down, and began to unwrap the silverware.

Watching, Dimaio became aware that an especially thick layer of grated Italian cheese lay across the top of the steaming spaghetti. An idea clicked in his brain. As Politz started to lift a generous helping to his mouth, Dimaio suddenly roused himself, staggered across the cell, and knocked the fork and spaghetti from Politz's hand.

"For God's sake, Joe," he whispered, "don't eat that. It's poisoned!"

Politz was stunned. Dramatically, Dimaio yanked Politz's plate toward him, rolled up a pinch of the cheese, and showed it to Politz. "I know poisons, Joe," he said. "That's arsenic."

Would the ruse work? Dimaio knew he had made the last, desperate throw of the dice. Either Politz would believe him —or he would be exposed and would be lucky to escape with his life.

Politz stared at Dimaio, bewildered and suspicious. Dimaio stared back at him, no sign of emotion on his face. Slowly, gingerly, Politz imitated Dimaio. He took a pinch of the heavy cheese, rolled it between his fingers, smelled it. Then he shook his head and pronounced his verdict. "Arsenic," he said.

Politz's nerves were now stretched almost to the snapping point. He began to pace up and down Dimaio's cell.

"Why would they want to poison me, Tony? Why? After all I have done for them," he said.

Softly, Dimaio asked: "What have you done, Joe?"

Politz sat down beside and whispered in Italian: "Murder, Tony. Murder, murder, murder."

Dimaio said nothing. This was not the moment to appear too eager. Let Politz stew.

And stew Politz did. All that night, he paced up and down his cell; it was nearly morning before he stretched out and fell asleep.

Dimaio, in the next few days, kept building up the pressure. He insisted on examining and carefully tasting every scrap of food before Politz ate it. He told a hair-raising fictitious story about an Italian woman of his grandmother's day. She had been used by the Mafia to poison landlords, he said; and he described in horrifying and minute detail the agonies suffered by her victims as the poison ate away the walls of their stomachs.

Politz became so unnerved at this recital that he jumped up and ran from Dimaio's cell, his hands over his ears. Dimaio was afraid that he might have gone too far. What if Politz lost all control over himself and began babbling to the other Mafiosi, screaming accusations at them? If that happened, Dimaio would certainly be killed before help could reach him. Fortunately, Politz, shaken though he was, retained sufficient presence of mind to keep silent, and Dimaio breathed a little easier. But he decided never to mention again the fictitious grandmother and her poisoning friend.

Only one final push was needed to drive Politz over the brink that would lead to confession, and Dimaio was becoming so weak that he knew he would have to deliver that final psychological shove at the soonest possible moment.

His opportunity came when Politz had another dinner and a bottle of wine delivered to the prison. Politz filled two wineglasses and passed one to Dimaio. The detective took a sip, then spat and hurled the wine-filled glass from him. Politz's eyes asked a horrified question. Dimaio nodded. "Cyanide, Joe," he whispered.

This final bit of play acting broke down Politz. Dimaio persuaded Weems, his regular cellmate, to sleep in Politz's cell that night, and Politz stayed with him. Politz was now completely unnerved, and Dimaio began to ply him with probing questions. Finally, in the early morning hours, Politz told all.

"We murdered Hennessy," he said.

Once he started talking, the details came pouring out of him in a flood. The names of those involved, the identity of witnesses, the name of the fourteen-year-old boy who had whistled *"La Marcia Reale"* ("The Royal March") as a signal that Hennessy was approaching—all of these facts and others tumbled from Politz's lips. Dawn was breaking before the talkative gangster fell into an exhausted sleep.

Dimaio now had the information he had suffered so long to get; his next task was to get out of prison and convey the details to Pinkerton. In this moment of triumph, with only one last hurdle before him, he suffered a stunning setback. The new attorney who had been hired to represent him quit. The lawyer told Pinkerton that the sight of the nineteen Mafiosi in the cellblock unnerved him—and well it might. For, only two days previously, a potential witness in the Hennessy case had been murdered in most gory fashion, his body butchered like that of a steer in a slaughterhouse and the remains dragged up to the roof of the police station, where they were left. This grim warning had apparently made a deep impression on the attorney.

Without a lawyer to get him out, Dimaio was now in a truly desperate situation. He was so weak that his head spun dizzily when he tried to stand up. He *had* to get word to Pinkerton somehow. Taking a chance, he used the last money he had to bribe a guard to send a telegram for him. It read: "Harry Minster, Attorney at Law, Chicago. Can you get me a writ? Tony."

Would the guard simply pocket the money? Or would he

fulfill his half of the deal and send the telegram? Dimaio could not tell. He could only wait.

Fortunately, the bribed guard kept his promise and the next morning a young French attorney called at the prison to see Dimaio. A writ of habeas corpus was issued, and the word got around the prison that Dimaio was to be released. In the cell-block, there was great rejoicing. Millionaire Charlie Matranga and Romero bribed the guards to bring in a farewell feast; the madam whose donations of food and wine had helped to save Dimaio's life contributed a couple of bottles of her best champagne; and Billy Weems gave "Tony, the counterfeiter" the names of all his New York underworld contacts to look up when he got out of prison.

When Dimaio finally left the horror house in which he had spent four months, he found Minster waiting for him in a carriage outside the prison gates. Minster took one look at him and was stunned. "My God, man, what has happened to you?" he asked.

"I guess I lost a few pounds," Dimaio told him—and fainted.

Minster hurried Dimaio to the hotel room where William Pinkerton was waiting. Pinkerton was as shocked as Minster had been at Dimaio's appearance and wanted to put him to bed immediately. But Dimaio refused. He insisted on getting the story Politz had told him on the record while every detail was fresh and sharp in his mind. A stenographer was called in, and Dimaio, interrupting his recital only to eat some of the nourishing food Pinkerton provided, dictated for hours.

District Attorney Charles J. Luzenberg, listening to the story Dimaio unfolded, was ecstatic.

"This could be the end of them," he told Pinkerton.

The district attorney sent out notices to convene the grand jury the next day.

"Do you think you're strong enough to testify?" he asked Dimaio.

"Give me a few hours' rest and another supper," the detective told him.

The following afternoon, Dimaio testified for four hours before the grand jury. Then exhaustion overcame him and he fell asleep in the witness chair. The next day, he finished his testimony, warning the jury that Politz had bragged the Mafia had unlimited funds and power, enough money and muscle to buy or intimidate any trial jury that could be drawn in New Orleans.

Dimaio offered to testify at the trial, but Luzenberg refused. "He will not live to leave the city if he takes the stand," the prosecutor told Pinkerton.

Dimaio was sent back to Philadelphia, where he was placed under a physician's care, and in New Orleans Luzenberg went ahead with the trial. He had built a seemingly ironclad case, calling a procession of witnesses, each of whom had bits of knowledge that fitted together like a mosaic. The impact of this testimony was capsuled in *Frank Leslie's Illustrated Newspaper* for April 4, 1891, in these words:

"Convinced as were the people of the guilt of the accused, they were staggered by the strength of the case made out by the State. Eye witnesses to the killing came forward and identified many of the men on trial. Circumstantial evidence of the most conclusive sort was piled on top of this . . . In the midst of the trial, Politz . . . broke down and confessed that he was present at the meeting of the society when the death of Hennessy was decreed, and when the detail of murderers was made. He gave a partial list of the members, and gave their signs and signals. He confessed that Macheca, one of the defendants, had furnished the 'Mafia guns' that were used, and had ordered him [Politz] to carry them to the house from which the assassins sallied when they killed Hennessy . . ."

Despite this testimony, the jury failed to convict when it got the case on March 12, 1891. The following day, the jury reported it had been unable to agree about the guilt of three —including even Politz, who had confessed all in open court —and it acquitted the others. The Mafia had indeed demonstrated that it could bribe or cow any jury in New Orleans.

There was no doubt about the bribery. The verdict had hardly been handed up when officials began to get evidence against Dominick O'Malley, the private detective whom Dimaio had named as a conduit for Mafia cash. O'Malley and a half-dozen others were swiftly indicted for bribery, and most of them were later convicted.

In the meantime, New Orleans was a seething city. Much of the Italian community greeted the shameful decision in the Hennessy murder trial with wild rejoicing. Sicilians who owned stands in the French Market bedecked them with bunting and streamers, and the Mafiosi, still held in prison on a lesser conspiracy charge, celebrated their courtroom victory with a bibulous party. At the lugger landing on the waterfront, a gang of Sicilians tore down the American flag, trampled it in the mud, and hoisted it upside down below the Italian banner. All over New Orleans, authorities were told,

Sicilians were bragging: "The Mafia is on top now and will run the town to suit itself."

These excesses, coming on the heels of the jobbing of justice in the courtroom, produced an inevitable counterexcess. A mass meeting was called for 10 A.M. on March 14. The notice for the rally was signed by sixty-one of New Orleans' leading citizens. Its announced purpose was "to remedy the failure of justice in the HENNESSY CASE." And it concluded with these ominous words: "Come prepared for action."

The mob that gathered in response to this call was in an aroused and ugly mood. Speakers announced the intention: they were going to march on the Old Parish Prison and execute the Mafiosi who had defied justice. The crowd roared its approval. Ranks were formed, and the vigilante army marched to a Canal Street gunstore, where they seized rifles and shotguns. Thus armed, they descended in overwhelming numbers upon the prison.

Guards were helpless. A door was smashed in and the search begun for the cowering Mafiosi. William S. Parkerson, the leader of the raiders, had drawn up a meticulous plan of action. The lynchers were to seek out just those eleven Italians whose guilt, to all reasonable men, had been established during the trial. They were not to touch others, like Millionaire Charlie Matranga, against whom the evidence had been less conclusive.

These orders were followed to the letter. Seven of the hunted eleven were gunned down in the women's yard of the prison. Two were found crouched in "the dog house," a large box under the stairs where the warden's bull terrier had been kept. They were riddled with bullets in their hideaway. Politz was dragged from the prison, shot, and hanged from a lamp-post. Another of the defendants, found shamming death under the pile of corpses in the women's yard, was hauled out and hanged from a tree in front of the prison. The grisly deed was completed; it had taken just an hour.

Parkerson climbed up on a window sill and called out to the mob that their mission had been accomplished. A few minutes later, when he marched his men out of the prison, he was hoisted onto the shoulders of his followers, much like a victorious football coach, and was carried through the streets of the city with thousands cheering his name.

No investigation was ever made of the lynching. Mayor Shakespear expressed the overwhelming popular sentiment when he said: "I do consider that the act was—however deplorable—a necessity and justifiable. The Italians had taken the law into their own hands and we had to do the same."

The power of the Mafia was broken for the time being in New Orleans, and it would be many long years before the secret society could reassert itself there.

As for Dimaio—"that wonderful detective," as William Pinkerton called him—his health was nearly broken by his long ordeal in the Old Parish Prison. Pinkerton sent him to Atlantic City to recuperate in the sea air, but it was almost a year before he was well enough to return to duty in the Philadelphia office.

Time and again during the early 1900s, he proved the nemesis of the Mafia, breaking up extortion rings in Columbus and Akron, Ohio. He retired in 1934, and in the late 1940s, when Jim Horan found him, he was living quietly in a hotel in Dover, Delaware, a gracious and alert gentleman of eighty-seven who liked to talk about some of his later duels with the Mafia.

He had become a legend in the agency in his own lifetime, and he chuckled as he confirmed the story of a famous encounter with the Mafiosi in Columbus. The secret society, which had come to dread and hate him because he had trapped so many of its members, made elaborate plans to murder him and his whole family by bombing his house. An informer tipped off Dimaio. The detective was enraged. Casting aside all caution, he stalked into a downtown Columbus grocery store owned by a member of the mob. Several of the gangsters were sitting around, drinking.

Drawing his revolver, Dimaio marched directly up to the man whom he knew to be the boss.

"Know who I am?" he demanded.

The Mafioso shook his head.

Dimaio poked the barrel of his gun almost up the boss's nostrils.

"I'm Dimaio," he said, "and the next time I hear anything about my house being bombed there's a Dago going to hell without a High Mass."

Then he turned and strode out of the store. His boldness, the suddenness of his action, had taken the mobsters so by surprise that they let him go. A few days later, Dimaio's informant told him that the secret society had called another meeting. It had decided it would be "a mistake" to bomb Dimaio's house.

11

An Image
Like the FBI

THE PINKERTONS in their heyday wore a halo that can only be compared to that of the Federal Bureau of Investigation and its late director, J. Edgar Hoover. In the public mind, they were idols of law enforcement—heroes in their homeland and internationally respected as the foremost detectives of their day.

Whenever William Pinkerton visited London, Scotland Yard, England's famous police agency, rolled out the red carpet and honored him at an elaborate banquet. This was in tribute to the man whose aid and advice the Yard frequently sought in tracking down counterfeiters, forgers, and international con men. Similarly, in America, local and state authorities turned almost automatically to the Pinkertons for assistance when they were confronted with an especially horrifying or difficult crime.

William and Robert Pinkerton, aided by the band of exceptional detectives they had lured into the agency, built such a reputation for skill, knowledge, and incorruptibility that many a case was broken almost by reputation alone. A couple of the agency's more remarkable achievements illustrate the point.

Former Governor Frank Steunenberg was walking to his home in Caldwell, Idaho, about six o'clock on the evening of December 30, 1905. He opened the front gate leading up the walk to his house—and was instantly blown to pieces by a bomb activated by a trip wire attached to the gate.

The murder of the former governor shocked state and nation. The deed stemmed, as was instantly apparent, from the long-running, savage warfare in western mining sections—a warfare that, as in the case of the Molly Maguires, was the almost inevitable result of the brutal, subhuman conditions imposed upon miners by mine owners.

Steunenberg, a Democrat, had been elected governor of Idaho in 1896. At the time of his murder, he had been a private citizen and sheep grower for five years, but the violence-prone Western Federation of Miners had never forgiven him for using force, as governor, to put down a mine strike.

The entire western mining country, embracing the states of Colorado, Nevada, Utah, and Idaho, had become a veritable battleground as mine owners paid starvation wages, refused to install safety devices, brought in strikebreakers, and used their wealth and political clout to crush attempts at union organization. The callousness and ruthlessness of the mine owners had provoked a wave of violence in which bombings, murders, and destruction of mine properties became almost daily occurrences. When striking miners set fire to the huge mine works at Wardner and left them in flaming ruins, Governor Steunenberg had felt he had to act. He had appealed to President William McKinley to send in federal troops to end the violence and lawlessness, an action hailed by the mine owners and one that incurred for the governor the undying enmity of the Western Federation of Miners.

The union publication, ironically named *Humanity,* hailed the murder of Steunenberg in these savage and inhuman terms: "Former Governor Frank Steunenberg of Idaho met his death last Saturday night at his home in Caldwell, Idaho. The press dispatches report his dissolution via the bomb route."

State and local authorities began an investigation. The local sheriff gathered up pieces of the exploded bomb and a piece of fishing line that had evidently been attached to the gate to trip the device. But the murder investigation, as is so often the case, seemed unable to fix upon any particular suspect.

At this point, the wildest of wild chances came to the aid of authorities. Sheriff Harvey K. Brown, of Baker County, Oregon, happened to go to Caldwell on an entirely unrelated investigation. On New Year's Day, 1906, he was passing the Saratoga Hotel when he caught a glimpse of a face he recognized.

"I know that fellow," he told the local sheriff. "He says his name is Hogan, but it isn't. He is Harry Orchard who used to be active in the miners' union in the Coeur d'Alene."

Orchard's room in the hotel was searched at once. In it, investigators found a length of fishing line identical to that used to set off the bomb; and in a trunk that Orchard had cached at the Caldwell railroad depot, they found dynamite, a sawed-off shotgun, and a collection of burglars' tools. The evidence clearly pointed to Orchard as the murderer, and he was soon arrested.

Governor Frank R. Gooding, like practically everyone else in authority, was convinced that Orchard had not acted on his own initiative, but had been the paid tool of the Western Federation. After some initial confusion and delay, telegrams were sent to the Pinkertons, urging the agency to come into the state and help develop the case against the higher-ups in the bomb plot.

As a result, there soon appeared upon the scene the manager of the agency's western division—none other than James McParland, the hero of the Molly Maguire investigation. McParland persuaded Governor Gooding and local magistrates to transfer Orchard to the state penitentiary in Boise. He summed up his thinking, as he had explained it to Idaho officials, in this manner:

"Place him in a cell in Murderers Row . . . Place guards who will watch him day and night, who will never take their eyes off him, either day or night—at the same time never speaking to him, nor to allow him any visitors except his lawyer. Keep the death watch on him for about three days and nights after which I will make an attempt to get a confession from him . . ."

McParland's recommendations were carried out, and the psychological warfare designed to break down Orchard began. Orchard's meals were handed to him in complete silence. When he asked a question, he didn't even get a grunt in reply. He wasn't permitted to see a newspaper or have any other reading material.

After several days of this nerve-wearing treatment, a guard

came to Orchard's cell—and suddenly spoke to him. Orchard was wanted, the guard said, in the warden's office. There the prisoner found a stranger sitting at the warden's desk, and the warden, after telling Orchard the man wanted to talk to him, walked out and left them alone.

The visitor whom Orchard saw was about sixty years old. He had thinning, grayish strands of hair that looked as if it had once been red. He had a flourishing walrus mustache and wore gold-rimmed spectacles. He was impeccably dressed like a gentleman of substance and carried a heavy black walking cane.

Orchard naturally wanted to know what the stranger wanted with him. The visitor said bluntly that he was not interested in Orchard personally, but in larger issues of law and order. According to McParland's later report, he told Orchard he had come "not to find out whether he was guilty, and we had positive proof and would hang him, but as he was but the tool of the inner circle, the hanging of him would be little satisfaction and [since he was only a tool] he, to a great extent, had my sympathy."

As the detective talked, a suspicion flickered in Orchard's mind.

"You're James McParland of the Pinkertons, aren't you?" he asked suddenly.

McParland replied: "I am. And I have come to give you some good advice."

Orchard, one of the most hardened killers the western mining country had spawned, replied contemptuously that he didn't need any advice. McParland talked on as if Orchard hadn't spoken. His talk took a religious turn. He mentioned

God and the glory of Heaven. He must have been quite elo-
quet, for the hardened Orchard, impressed, admitted a bit
shamefacedly that he didn't know much about God but
guessed He must be up there somewhere. McParland nodded
understandingly, tapped the killer on the shoulder as a father
might his son, and took his leave, having scored enough points
for one day.

There followed daily sessions in the warden's office. The evidence indicates that Orchard was greatly impressed (he may
even have felt honored) to be receiving such personal attention from the great James McParland, whose feats in the
Molly Maguire case had made him a famous personage in
the West. On one occasion, Orchard asked McParland why
he hadn't pursued Thomas Hurley, one of the Mollies who
was then in Gunnison jail on a minor charge. McParland
replied promptly: "Because Hurley was a tool of Jack Kehoe
as you are of Haywood."

The Haywood to whom McParland referred was "Big
Bill" Haywood, a one-eyed, powerful giant. Haywood was
the toughest and most ruthless labor leader of his time, a man
committed to the principle of all-out class warfare; and when
he died years later, his bones were interred in the Kremlin in
Moscow. At the time of Steunenberg's murder, Haywood dominated the miners' union and was the boss of a triumvirate
whose other members were Charles A. Pettibone and Charles
H. Moyer.

Orchard made no response to McParland's initial suggestion that Haywood had been using him as "a tool." The
detective didn't press the point. He left the seed to take root
while he continued to talk about God and religion, assuring

Orchard that there was no crime for which God would not forgive him if he truly repented. There is even a legend that McParland had an organ moved in Orchard's cellblock so that the prison silence could be broken by the strains of hymns familiar at frontier revival meetings.

In some of his reports, McParland outlined his persuasive methods in these words:

"I said to Orchard that a man of his intelligence and reasoning power, as his forehead would indicate, had the ability of doing a large amount of good as well as evil. If he had not started out with anarchists and murderers he could have been a shining light . . ."

McParland kept impressing upon Orchard that the lawyers furnished him by the miners' federation were there to protect the higher-ups, not Orchard. They would, McParland argued, "fool him up to the time he took his journey from cell to scaffold."

Orchard—filled with this new image of himself as a "shining light" if others had not led him astray, moved by McParland's brand of religious evangelism, convinced he was being used as a sucker by the higher-ups, finally broke in the last week of January and began to tell all. Though Orchard had never previously been arrested, he confessed to McParland that he killed some thirty men. He described how he had planted a bomb deep in the Vindicator Mine, then being worked by nonunion laborers, and how the bomb had gone off, taking such an enormous toll of life that "Haywood and Pettibone were well pleased and thought it was a good job and the officers [of the mine union] were all elected and nobody had any kick coming." Orchard said he was paid three hundred dollars by Pettibone.

According to Orchard's confession, the Steunenberg murder had been arranged and paid for by Haywood, Pettibone, and Moyer. Haywood, he said, had thought the murder would terrorize current public officials, "telling them they were not forgotten" and condemning them, even after they left office, to "a living death, thinking they had an assassin on their trail at all times."

As he obtained this horrifying confession from Orchard, McParland warned: "It is absolutely necessary to corroborate Orchard's testimony as to his travels from the time he first reached Idaho until the time of the assassination."

The Pinkertons set out to do just this, and their researches left little room for doubt that Orchard was telling the truth. Point after point checked out just as he had said it would. An accomplice of Orchard's in various murders and in the early trailing of Steunenberg had been a man by the name of Steve Adams. The Pinkertons tracked down Adams and got a confession from him, corroborating Orchard's. Haywood, Pettibone, and Moyer were arrested and brought to Idaho for trial.

The case that had looked so ironclad began to spring leaks. The miner's union raised $300,000 and hired Clarence Darrow, who was to become the most famous criminal trial lawyer of his day, to represent Haywood in the first murder trial. Darrow, working through a relative of Adams', induced the accomplice to repudiate his confession. McParland, furious, tried to get Adams to recant this recantation, but in this even the persuasive Pinkerton detective failed. Adams' desertion blew a disastrous hole in the state's case because it was just about impossible to convict a man on the word of a lone accomplice; corroboration of Orchard's confession was needed. And, with Adams' desertion, this corroboration had been removed.

Added to this was the eloquence of Darrow. He pictured the prosecution as far more than a murder case—indeed, as part of a vast antiunion conspiracy. He summed up for eleven hours, eulogizing American labor and pillorying the evils of the capitalistic system whose excesses and brutality at the time furnished him with much devastating ammunition. Thus, in the end, Darrow prevailed, and Haywood, Pettibone, and Moyer were freed. Only Orchard was convicted and sentenced to a life term in prison.

Yet anyone who reads the Pinkerton reports, which show how Orchard's confession was backed up by minute detail after detail, has to come away from the case convinced that a classic jobbing of justice was performed in the courtroom. Though the Pinkertons had not prevailed, James McParland had again demonstrated their ability to crack even the toughest of rogues. It was a feat achieved not only by McParland's astute psychological maneuvers but because, quite simply, he was James McParland, a man who was considered a straight shooter on his side of the law and one who had earned the respect of even the criminals whom he hunted.

This same curious respect of the professional criminal for his professional opposite provided the stimulus that enabled the Pinkertons to solve the greatest art theft of the Victorian age —a deed that had baffled Scotland Yard for twenty-five years.

The principal actors in this drama were physical and ethical opposites—six-foot tall, powerfully built William Pinkerton and the slight, dapper Adam Worth, the greatest criminal brain of his day. Worth was only five feet six inches tall and never weighed more than about a hundred and thirty pounds. He had unusually long, well-muscled arms for a man of his slight stature. He had large, bright, extremely dark eyes; thick black hair and luxurious sideburns; and a sad, sober face that made him look more like a professor than the tough criminal he was. Yet this was the man who, in a thirty-five year criminal career, stole an estimated $4 million—and, in addition, in one of his boldest strokes, made off with a bit of loot that was worthless to him, the priceless but unmarketable Gainsborough painting of the "Duchess of Devonshire."

Even as a young man barely into his twenties, Worth was noted for his patience and meticulous planning. He would devote weeks, even months, to the study of a particular job, devising the safest and surest way of making off with the loot. He abhorred violence and never committed bloodshed. His was a criminal career that always emphasized brains over brawn.

His only arrest in the United States came in 1864, when he was seized in New York for the theft of a package from an express truck and sentenced to serve three years in Sing Sing. New York's famous prison held him for only eighteen months before he made a daring escape and embarked upon a career that was to baffle the police of three continents. Worth began this career of crime in the Boston area in 1867.

His first big strike, which he pulled off alone, was the theft of $20,000 from an insurance company safe in Cambridge, Massachusetts. Flush with cash, Worth, who was always something of a dandy, bought himself an expensive wardrobe and took up residence in the Astor House, which he later described to William Pinkerton as "the only first-class hotel in New York."

Now he began to gather about him a ring of crooks for his next major foray, the cracking of the huge iron safe in the Boylston National Bank in Boston. To get into the bank, Worth and his principal accomplice, Charles Bullard, bought an adjoining barbershop and converted the store to a "wine shop," decorating their window with an attractive display of bottles. All the time, behind a partition, they quietly chipped away at the brick and mortar that separated their "business" from the bank. Finally, on the night of November 22, 1869, while a storm raged over Boston, they made their final breakthrough, blew the bank's safe, and scooped some $450,000 in cash and negotiable securities into carpet bags.

The securities were "worked back" through underworld fences at some 10 to 25 per cent of their real value. Even so, the haul bankrolled Worth and Bullard and set them up in style as gentlemen of means and leisure. They promptly boarded a steamer for England. There, they knew, they would be safe from prosecution as there were no international extradition laws covering bank robbery at that time.

From the moment they landed in Liverpool, the handsome pair of rogues cut a swath across all levels of British society. On their first night in the pub of the American Hotel, they met an enchantress, a beautiful barmaid named Kitty Flynn. Underworld accomplices said later that Adam Worth had fallen hopelessly in love with Kitty; but Kitty—attracted by the taller and more imposing, but less stable and less clever, Bullard—chose the wrong man.

After Bullard and Kitty left for a honeymoon in Paris, Worth took out his frustration on an unsuspecting pawnbroker. He purloined the keys to the man's vault, had them duplicated, and returned them before they could be missed. Then, on an appropriately dark night, he let himself into the vault and made off with loot valued at 20,000 British pounds, or, in the exchange of the time, roughly 100,000 American dollars. There was a great hue and cry in Liverpool. Worth, too canny to give himself away by a sudden departure, loitered about the city for some weeks, grave, professional, dignified. Then he departed for London.

In the British capital, he established himself in lodgings at 158 Piccadilly, with prime ministers, lords, artists, and the elite of British society as neighbors. Using the alias of Henry J. Raymond—the name of a famous editor of the New York *Times*—Worth mingled in the best circles on the one hand and, on the other, established himself as the brains of an international band of con men and thieves.

Back in America, the Pinkertons had not been idle. They had identified Worth and Bullard as the principal architects of the Boylston bank job, but they could not touch the pair as long as they stayed in England. The Pinkertons had, however, good connections with Scotland Yard, and they regularly transmitted to the Yard all the information they gathered on the ring of American thieves in London.

Bullard and Worth moved on to Paris, where they invested some $75,000 (an enormous amount in those days) in furnishing the first splendiferous American nightclub in the

French capital. While Kitty charmed the customers, Worth, Bullard, and their associates fleeced the suckers in a second-floor gambling casino. William Pinkerton, following the trail of American bank robbers who had fled abroad, heard about this plush American Bar and decided to visit it. Worth spotted him the moment he entered and nudged Bullard. "Billy Pinkerton," he whispered.

Bullard hastened to carry the alarm to various crooks and their floozies in the faro room upstairs while Worth greeted Pinkerton courteously and invited him to the bar for a drink. It was the beginning of a strange relationship—and the beginning of the end, too, for the American Bar. Pinkerton and Superintendent John Shore of Scotland Yard put united pressure on the French authorities to clamp down on the nightclub that had become the rendezvous for international criminals. The French were reluctant to move because Worth had, of course, greased many palms, but the combined pressure of the Pinkertons and the Yard was too much. Ward and Bullard had to sell their nightclub and return to London.

There followed years of incredible adventures and fantastic heists. Bullard landed in jail, and Worth and Kitty became a domestic twosome. Their idyl lasted only until Bullard reappeared upon the scene and once more mesmerized Kitty. Worth appears to have been devastated by her desertion (her two daughters were said to have been his) and applied himself to ever more fantastic criminal forays.

On one occasion, when some of his accomplices were caught by Turkish police and lodged in the Constantinople prison, Worth journeyed to Turkey, a country with which he was entirely unfamiliar. He studied the scene, managed to get duplicate keys to the prison cellblock—and sprang his confederates. On another, he traveled to South Africa, and in an elaborate plot stole a fortune in uncut diamonds being shipped from the closely guarded Kimberley diamond mines. Back in London, he found himself a knowledgeable partner, became a "diamond merchant," and worked his untraceable loot back into the regular channels of trade.

There were, of course, some misfortunes. One of these occurred in May 1876, when Worth's bumbling brother, John, got himself arrested by British authorities. Worth knew that British prisons were more difficult to get out of than the one in Constantinople, and he was walking along Bond Street, cudgeling his brains to find some way of helping John, on the afternoon of May 27, 1876. He was accompanied by a huge, gorilla-like man named Jack Phillips, known as Junka. As the pair approached the art gallery of Agnew & Company, they noticed a long line of people queued up in the street. Worth inquired about the cause of such a crowd and was informed that Gainsborough's famous painting "Duchess of Devonshire" was on display. With the news came a flash of inspiration: Worth told Junka on the spot that he was going to steal the painting.

A Baltimore bank robber, Joseph Elliott, was contacted to serve as lookout, and the following night the trio returned to the gallery. London streets were shrouded with a dense fog that made the night ideal for Worth's purpose. Junka placed his enormous bulk against the wall of the building, and Worth, using the giant as a human ladder, climbed up on his shoulders, jimmied a window, and entered the second-floor art gallery. In minutes he had cut the "Duchess" from her frame, rolled up the canvas, and was climbing back to the ground on his Junka-ladder.

His purpose, as he later explained, was to rescue his brother. He had calculated on bargaining with British authorities. The deal: free John Worth and get back the Gainsborough.

When Worth called on his brother's attorney the day after the theft, however, he was astounded to find the man jubilant. The lawyer had discovered a technical flaw in the indictment against John Worth; John was to be freed. The theft of the Gainsborough had been unnecessary—and Adam Worth was left with an unmarketable white elephant on his hands.

He was left, too, with accomplices who posed threats to his own safety. Persuasive though he was, Adam Worth had difficulty convincing them that a priceless painting, just because it was unique and priceless, was worthless to the thieves who had taken it. He finally persuaded Elliott to go back to America, paying his passage, but the gorilla-like Junka was more troublesome. Worth paid Junka fifty British pounds, but Junka was soon back, demanding more.

The two went one night to the Criterion Bar, a popular rendezvous. There Junka became very abusive and demanding. The slight, frail Adam Worth looked helpless alongside his hulking companion, but he suddenly swung a haymaker from the floor, landing the punch squarely on Junka's jaw and knocking the giant out cold. A Scotland Yard detective, in the bar at the time, had to drag the infuriated Adam Worth away before he kicked the fallen Junka into the next world. The midget conqueror dusted off his hands and strolled out of the bar, untouched by the law or Junka.

It was during this period that Worth had the last of a series of encounters with William Pinkerton in England. Pinkerton was frequenting the Criterion Bar, and Worth tried to cultivate his acquaintance. The master criminal appears to have been strangely fascinated by the master detective who might well be his undoing. He conversed with Pinkerton and tried to offer him a number of presents, evidently hoping to gain his good will. Pinkerton, of course, refused the gifts, but he appears to have been entertained by Worth's maneuvers. And so, one night he "introduced" Worth to Superintendent Shore of Scotland Yard. Verbal fireworks followed.

Worth had a very low opinion of Shore. In addition, he was undoubtedly irritated because the Yard frequently stationed operatives at his very doorstep to spy on him. And so, in this face-to-face encounter, Worth exploded. He later recalled:

"I told Shore he didn't know anybody but a lot of three-card monte men and cheap pickpockets and he could thank the God Almighty the Pinkertons were his friends or he would never have gotten above an ordinary street detective."

Motivated by this detestation of Shore and the Yard on the one hand, his admiration of William Pinkerton on the other, Adam Worth sought out Pinkerton when he finally decided to try to return the stolen "Duchess of Devonshire." Worth's overture came at the end of a long career that had begun to run tragically downhill. The one real love of his life, Kitty Bullard, had finally separated from her unreliable husband, had gone to New York, and there—her beauty still remarkable—had gotten a divorce and married wealthy businessman Juan Terry. She became a society figure, her popularity undimmed by disclosure of her past, and entertained lavishly at

the Terry mansion in Long Branch, New Jersey. Worth had married "a little English girl" by whom he had a son and a daughter. But in 1892, in the only botched job of his career, he was arrested in Belgium and sentenced to seven years in prison. Released in 1897, he returned to London to find that his wife had been seduced by one of his criminal associates, had become a narcotics addict, and was confined in an asylum. His children had been sent to live with John Worth and his wife in Brooklyn. Bullard and several other former partners in crime had died, and Worth himself had contracted tuberculosis.

And so, knowing his end could not be far off, Adam Worth cautiously approached William Pinkerton about the return of the Gainsborough masterpiece. He had kept it carefully stored all those years in warehouses in Manhattan, Brooklyn, Boston, and Jersey City. His idea evidently was that the Pinkertons might collect a long-standing reward and split with him. William Pinkerton was having no part of any such deal, but he agreed to meet with Worth under a gentleman's agreement that nothing Worth said would be used against him.

The meeting took place in late 1898 in Pinkerton's Chicago office. Pinkerton explained that the agency, as a matter of policy, never accepted special rewards for its work. Worth nodded that he understood. "I am putting myself in your hands," he said.

The two men then sat and conversed companionably about Worth's criminal career. Worth talked freely about his foreign exploits. The only American charge that could be brought against him dealt with the old Boylston bank robbery—and

most of the witnesses in that case were dead. He knew that he had little to fear, and he trusted Pinkerton.

As for Pinkerton, he seemed to have formed a genuine liking for this genteel, fashionably dressed, soft-spoken rogue who was a genius on his own wrong side of the law. Pinkerton was also sorry for him—for his wasted and tragic life, and for the end that was so near (his tubercular cough shook him even as they talked).

This conference touched off a long and intricate chain of negotiations, the details of which are not clear. Pinkerton, it is obvious, communicated with Scotland Yard, and a number of messages passed back and forth. Finally, on January 16, 1901, the Yard advised Pinkerton to make a deal with Worth for the return of the Gainsborough. The bargain almost certainly included a guarantee that Worth would not be prosecuted in England, and there may even have been some promise of a cash payment to him.

In any event, a partner in the Agnew firm went to Chicago on March 27, 1901, twenty-five years, minus two months, from the time the Gainsborough masterpiece had been stolen. Pinkerton, who had contacted Worth, joined the British visitor in his hotel room. Soon there came a knock on the door, and a messenger handed in a package. It was a cylinder wrapped in ordinary brown wrapping paper. Pinkerton opened it and drew from the tube the lovely painting, unspoiled by the passage of time.

Shortly afterward, Adam Worth went off to Hot Springs, Arkansas, with William and Robert Pinkerton, apparently as their guest. A picture taken at the time shows him riding upright in a carriage, facing Robert Pinkerton, and one can

almost see the look of satisfaction on his face. The Pinkertons were now the only real friends he had, and he seemed to feel quite distinguished riding in their company—a lofty association that none of his criminal associates could ever possibly have achieved.

"If I can ever do you a favor on earth, outside of going right out and being a policeman, I want you to call on me," he told William Pinkerton.

In returning the Gainsborough, however, Adam Worth had performed his last and perhaps his only public service. He returned to London, ill and racked with his tubercular cough, and there he died on January 8, 1902.

12
The
Modern Agency

THE PINKERTONS no longer ride to glory in the headlines, as they did in the first seventy-five years of their history. They have been replaced in their role as the chief—indeed, at times, the only—skillful law-enforcement agency in the nation by professional city and state police departments and by such federal agencies as the FBI and the Bureau of Narcotics and Dangerous Drugs.

The modern agency, especially since the FBI began to come into prominence under J. Edgar Hoover in 1924, has increasingly devoted itself to guard and security services and to such specialized fields as the protection of the nation's racetracks. Fixers of horse races at leading tracks protected by the Pinkertons get the jitters knowing that The Eye will be upon them at the first suspicion of rigging. Jewel thieves are uncomfortably aware that the Pinkertons have protected the Jewelers' Security Alliance since the 1880s and that investigators of the agency will add their own expertise to that of constituted authorities any time there is a major jewel robbery.

Throughout the agency's history, there has been only one persistent and glaring flaw—its insensitivity (indeed, what seemed at times its callousness) in labor disputes. Its role in the Molly Maguire investigation, the Homestead shootout, and other labor wars of the 1880s and 1890s was severely criticized by union leaders. But perhaps the darkest hour came in its unabashed labor spying during the 1920s and 1930s. By 1936 some 30 per cent of the firm's business derived from so-called industrial services. These consisted primarily of placing opertives or undercover agents in industrial plants to spy on union organizing efforts and inform the owners about them.

This widespread activity made the Pinkertons the most hated and detested force in the nation in union circles. A Congressional investigation in 1936, during the heyday of President Franklin D. Roosevelt's reform administration, concentrated on the Pinkertons' labor-spying role. Robert A. Pinkerton, great-grandson of the founder and then head of the agency, defended the Pinkertons' record, arguing that an employer has a "right to know" what is going on in his plant. He also contended that evidence gained by the agency's industrial service unit had resulted in court convictions of some two thousand persons "guilty of such crimes as assaults, murders, arson, kidnaping, bombings and all types of criminal offenses in connection with labor disputes."

Much of big business was paranoid at the time—and some industrialists have remained so ever since—about the so-called "Communist menace." Many businessmen had visions of Communists lurking under almost every bed, ready to overthrow the capitalist system, and the Pinkertons appear to have been infected with this kind of bias. Their reports referred frequently to this supposed Communist threat; yet, ironically, if not comically, none of the officers of the agency, when questioned by the Congressional committee, could swear "to ever having seen a communist."

The Wagner Act and other reforms of the Roosevelt era gave labor the kind of protection it had not had in the days of Allan Pinkerton. It became illegal for an employer to fire a hired hand for indulging in union-organizing activity, and the law now frowned on the employment of armed goon squads to cow the workers and protect strikebreakers. These changes in the official climate brought a change, perhaps belated, in the attitude of the agency.

In April 1937, the Pinkerton board of directors passed a resolution putting an end to labor spying. In announcing the action, Robert Pinkerton acknowledged that "it looks as if we were on the wrong side of the fence. Times have changed and we were out of step." Later he amplified this by telling the New York *Times*, "That is a phase of our business that we are not particularly proud of and we're delighted we're out of it."

In areas involving pure detective work, the Pinkertons remained as skillful as they had been in the days of the founder. Time and again, in pursuing jewel thieves or racetrack fixers, they demonstrated that they had lost none of their ancient skills.

One of the agency's most famous cases in the 1930s exposed the king of racetrack ringers, Peter C. (Paddy) Barrie, an Irishman who had a genius for painting a nag to look like a champion or a fast horse to impersonate a nag. Barrie was a short, chubby individual with dark brown eyes and a flair for flashy clothes, expensive cars, and fast women.

He began his career in larceny as a sixteen-year-old stable-boy in England. He pretended to become excessively fond of a dapple-gray mare belonging to his employer, Lady Mary Cameron. So sincere seemed the love of boy for horse that Lady Mary finally let Paddy have the mare for about $85, half what she was worth. Paddy left with the dapple-gray, but four months later he showed up at Lady Mary's estate, informing his former employer that he had "gone into the horse business," as indeed he had, and exhibiting as proof a beautiful, frisky reddish-brown mare. The mare, he assured Lady Mary, was a real bargain; and she was so taken with the horse that she paid Paddy $1,500. Within a few days, the mare's reddish-brown coat began to fade back to its original dapple-gray, and it became obvious that Lady Mary had paid $1,500 for the nag she had sold Paddy for $85. It was Paddy's first "ringing," the name for such frauds among horsemen.

After World War I and a bout with Scotland Yard that earned him a brief tour in grim Dartmoor Prison, Paddy Barrie came to the United States, skipping illegally across the border from Canada. He worked at his horse-camouflaging art until he discovered dyes that would stick to an animal's coat for weeks and until he perfected a compound—composed of heroin, cola nut extract, glycerin, and strychnine—that juiced the sorriest nag into the delusion he was a Kentucky Derby winner.

Paddy Barrie, lacking money to make a killing from his finely perfected art, sought backers—and found them in underworld bosses always eager for a new racket to take the suckers to the cleaners. His first ringing at a Chicago track was not too successful because his ringer, unfortunately, was a horse that didn't like to run in the mud—and the track was muddy that day. There was some muttering among the mob chiefs about doing away with Paddy, but they finally decided there would be no profit in murder—and there might be a profit if Paddy was encouraged to try, try again.

They were so right. In 1931, Paddy purchased a swift three-year-old named Aknathon from the Marshall Field stables for $4,300. At about the same time, he laid out $400 for a dark sorrel named Shem, a nag with a record of invariably eating dust at the tail end of the pack. Barrie dyed Aknathon with such skill that the most experienced eye could not tell the two horses apart.

All was now ready for what proved to be Barrie's greatest coup. He pulled it off on October 3, 1931, at the Harve de Grace racetrack in Maryland, right under the eyes of Governor Albert C. Ritchie. Mrs. Payne Whitney's Byzantine was a heavy favorite to win the race, and few bettors paid any attention to the horse running as Shem. The odds on "Shem" were 52 to 1; but with Aknathon running in Shem's shoes as it were, Byzantine was left in the dust. The Pinkertons later estimated that Barrie's underworld backers cleaned up $1 million.

Unfortunately for Barrie, one unsavory character at the track didn't know how to keep his mouth shut. The braggart was a loud, swaggering New York racketeer known as "Nigger" Nate Raymond. Raymond had gone to the pari-mutuel windows at the last minute and plunked down a wad on Shem to win. When the ringer came in, Raymond cashed in his bet for $130,000, and he couldn't resist telling everyone within shouting distance how smart he was. "I had $2,500 down on that goat," he exulted. "Boy, can I pick 'em."

The thing smelled, and the Pinkertons sniffed the odor. They were already suspicious about the first ringing attempt in Chicago, but they had as yet no idea of the identity of the crooked genius who had perfected the art of altering the appearance of horses. While they hunted frantically for clues, Barry kept right on ringing, skipping about the nation from one track to another, with one venture south of the border, in Mexico.

He was aware that the Pinkertons were after him, but he changed his own appearance, altering the color of his hair and mustache as skillfully as he changed the coats of his horses. There were, however, tracks he couldn't cover. The Pinkertons traced the manner in which horses had been shipped; they discovered the stables in which they had been secreted between races; they learned that "Nigger" Nate Raymond had been seen frequently around New York in the company of a short, brown-eyed, chubby little man whom he called "Paddy." And this Paddy, they were told, spoke with an unmistakable English accent.

The Pinkertons wired this information to Scotland Yard and soon had an answer to their riddle. "Paddy" was identified as the same Peter Christian (Paddy) Barrie who had swindled Lady Cameron in the case of the dapple-gray. From that point on, Paddy Barrie's number was up, though it still took the Pinkertons some time to catch up with him.

Doggedly, they tracked Barrie from ringing to ringing, and finally in 1932, they located him in Miami. Immigration authorities, tipped by the Pinkertons, stepped in and held the master ringer for extradition. But Paddy, admitted to bail, skipped from his hotel in the deep of night and was on the loose again.

Once more, the Pinkertons took up the chase, but it was not until August 1934 that Pinkerton aces, protecting the famous Saratoga track in upstate New York, got the break for which they had been waiting. They spotted a flashily dressed, beautiful woman whom they had suspected of being associated with Barrie in one of his previous ringings. They followed the woman, and she led them to Barrie, sitting behind the wheel of a horse van, about to drive a nag away.

For Paddy that, truly, was the end of the line. There was no bail for him this time, and a Pinkerton operative followed him right on board the White Star liner Caledonia on November 3, 1934, just to make certain Paddy was really on his way back to his native England.

One effect of Paddy Barrie's fraudulent career was the development of tighter methods of control at racetracks the Pinkertons protected. Each horse running at a Pinkerton-protected track is given a number, and the number is tattooed on the horse's inner upper lip. Detailed descriptions of every animal—including his color, markings, traits, and physical peculiarities—are kept in Pinkerton files. Close-up photographs are taken of a horse's four "nighteyes," the scaly, hardened skin on the inner side of each leg. These never change and are the equine counterpart of the human fingerprint. Such protective methods make ringing practically impossible at Pinkerton-guarded tracks.

Paddy Barrie wasn't the only crooked genius to find the

Pinkertons too much for him. In protecting firms represented by the Jewelers' Security Alliance, the Pinkertons matched wits with another master criminal—Willie (the Actor) Sutton, the foremost bank robber of his day.

The Pinkertons' long affair with Sutton began on October 28, 1930, when the fashionable New York jewelry firm of M. Rosenthal & Sons was robbed of some $129,000 in gems. It happened before opening time. A wispy little man with a hound-dog sad face, dressed in the uniform of a Postal Telegraph messenger, came to the door, flourishing a telegram. A porter, unsuspecting, unlocked the door and let him in. The phony messenger was Sutton, and the porter was soon bound and gagged. As other employees of the firm appeared for work one by one, Sutton and his partner, Marcus Bassett, quickly trussed them up and went on with their task of cracking and looting the safe. Then they bade their helpless prisoners a polite good morning and vanished into crowds along the street.

The technique was one that Sutton was to use over and over again, hence his nickname, Willie the Actor. In the Rosenthal case, the Pinkertons spent three months checking thousands of messenger boys until they finally found the one who had sold Willie his uniform. With some clue to his identity but none to his whereabouts, they questioned hundreds of additional witnesses until they located one who recalled part of the license number of a car in which he had seen Willie. Tracking down this slim clue required a study of countless license plate numbers issued in the five boroughs of New York City before the Pinkertons finally found one to a car that belonged to a girl friend of Willie's.

It had been backbreaking, tedious, boring work—a procedure far removed from the glamorous excitement of detective tales on television—but it led in the end to Pinkerton detectives trapping Willie and his girl friend as they sat engaged in deep conversation in a Broadway cafeteria.

Willie the Actor was sent to Sing Sing, but prison couldn't hold him. He escaped a year later and went right back to plying his old trade of robbery. Willie drove police of several states almost out of their minds as he knocked over bank after bank. Almost invariably, he gained admittance by posing in some kind of uniform, as a messenger, a postman, or a policeman. It was not until the early 1950s that Willie's career came to an end. He robbed a Long Island bank, still using the technique the Pinkertons had identified twenty years earlier. He made off with his loot successfully enough, but he was trapped some months later when a passer-by recognized him while he was changing the battery in his car on a Brooklyn Street.

Such, then, is the record of the Pinkertons. The agency, which had been privately owned from the day of its founding, went public with the issuance of stock in 1967 and is now known as Pinkerton's, Inc., instead of Pinkerton's National Detective Agency. In this same year, the agency was headed for the first time by someone other than a Pinkerton. Edward J. Bednarz, who had joined the firm as a special racetrack agent in 1947, became the first non-Pinkerton chief.

Time has brought many changes since the agency was founded nearly a hundred twenty-five years ago. The Pinkerton role is less glamorous today than it was in decades past when law enforcement was in its infancy. But Pinkerton's remains the most famous of all private detective agencies in the nation, and it still on occasion renders invaluable assistance to regularly constituted law enforcement authorities in tracking down criminals who are so foolhardy as to challenge it in areas of its special concerns.

INDEX

Pettibone, Charles A., 150–53 *passim*

Philadelphia office, Pinkerton's, 124, 125

Phillips, Jack (Junka), 158–59

Pinkerton, Allan: precautions of, to thwart assassination plots against Pres. Lincoln, 1–11 *passim;* physical description of, 1, 14–15, 47; railroads and express agencies, protection of, by, 3, 26, 29, 73; date and place of birth, 13; parents and brother of, 13–14; slum upbringing of, 14; traits and characteristics of, 14, 16, 22; as young cooper, 14–15, 17, 19–22 *passim;* as violent rebel and Chartist, 15–17, 32, 66; marriage of, to Joan Carfrae, 17; beginnings of career as a detective, 19–24; activities of, in Dundee, 19–21, 24, 25, 30; corralling counterfeiters, 21, 23–25 *passim;* accepts deputyship in Chicago, 25; founding of his detective agency in Chicago, 25–32; shot by gunman, 27; as abolitionist, 30; as spy for the Union, 33–39; surveillance and downfall of Rebel Rose, due to actions of, 42, 46–60 *passim;* as Union spy master, 61–66; raid on Knights of Liberty, directed by, 62–63; takes field with McClellan's Army, 65–66; tracking of desperadoes by, 69–95; on trail of Reno brothers gang, 73–95; attempts on life of, 89–90; boat "accident" of, while transporting prisoners, 90–91; meeting with the governor, after New Albany lynchings, 94; near-fatal stroke of, and return to Chicago by, 97–

99; role of, in labor strife, 97–117 *passim;* Chicago fire, wiping out headquarters of, 98–99; prosecution of the Molly Maguires by, 99–117 *passim;* protection of property by, in seventy strikes, 116; death of, 123

Pinkerton, Allan, grandfather of Allan Pinkerton, 13, 14

Pinkerton, Isabella McQueen, mother of Allan Pinkerton, 13–14

Pinkerton, Joan Carfrae, wife of Allan Pinkerton, 17, 19, 25, 30

Pinkerton, Robert, brother of Allan Pinkerton, 14

Pinkerton, Robert, son of Allan Pinkerton, 70, 97, 123–25, 145–46, 162

Pinkerton, Robert A., great-grandson of the founder, 166, 167

Pinkerton, William, father of Allan Pinkerton, 13–14

Pinkerton, William, son of Allan Pinkerton, 31, 32, 67, 75–80 *passim,* 90, 94, 97, 123, 124–43 *passim,* 145–46, 154–63 *passim*

"Pinkerton Kid" (Pat O'Neil), 87, 88

Pinkerton mine squad, 109

Pinkertons, and the Mafia, 119–43 *passim*

Pinkerton's, Inc.: guidelines for, 28–29; issuance of public stock by, 173

Pinkerton's National Detective Agency: destruction of, in Chicago fire, 98–99; now known as Pinkerton's, Inc., 173

Police departments, seeking aid of Pinkerton, 123

Politz, Emanuel (Polizzi), 129

THE AUTHOR

FRED COOK is a graduate of Rutgers University. He is a newspaperman of vast experience as well as a free-lance writer. He is the author of over twenty-five books and numerous magazine articles for *Reader's Digest*, *American Heritage*, and the New York Sunday *Times Magazine*. He won Page One Awards from the New York Newspaper Guild in 1958, 1959, and 1960 and the Sidney Hillman Award in 1961.